T0140358

Studies in Computational Intelligence   1092

Series Editor

Janusz Kacprzyk, *Polish Academy of Sciences, Warsaw, Poland*

The series "Studies in Computational Intelligence" (SCI) publishes new developments and advances in the various areas of computational intelligence—quickly and with a high quality. The intent is to cover the theory, applications, and design methods of computational intelligence, as embedded in the fields of engineering, computer science, physics and life sciences, as well as the methodologies behind them. The series contains monographs, lecture notes and edited volumes in computational intelligence spanning the areas of neural networks, connectionist systems, genetic algorithms, evolutionary computation, artificial intelligence, cellular automata, self-organizing systems, soft computing, fuzzy systems, and hybrid intelligent systems. Of particular value to both the contributors and the readership are the short publication timeframe and the world-wide distribution, which enable both wide and rapid dissemination of research output.

Indexed by SCOPUS, DBLP, WTI Frankfurt eG, zbMATH, SCImago.

All books published in the series are submitted for consideration in Web of Science.

Rafik Hadfi · Reyhan Aydoğan · Takayuki Ito ·
Ryuta Arisaka

Editors

Recent Advances in Agent-Based Negotiation: Applications and Competition Challenges

 Springer

Editors
Rafik Hadfi
Department of Social Informatics
Kyoto University
Kyoto, Japan

Reyhan Aydoğan
Computer Science
Özyeğin University
Alemdağ, Turkey

Takayuki Ito
Department of Social Informatics
Kyoto University
Kyoto, Japan

Ryuta Arisaka
Department of Social Informatics
Kyoto University
Kyoto, Japan

ISSN 1860-949X   ISSN 1860-9503 (electronic)
Studies in Computational Intelligence
ISBN 978-981-99-0563-8   ISBN 978-981-99-0561-4 (eBook)
https://doi.org/10.1007/978-981-99-0561-4

This Springer imprint is published by the registered company Springer Nature Singapore Pte Ltd.
The registered company address is: 152 Beach Road, #21-01/04 Gateway East, Singapore 189721, Singapore

About the Book

In agent-based negotiations, intelligent software agents negotiate with their human or software counterparts to reach agreements in any domain. Negotiation agents have been widely studied in the field of multi-agent systems and artificial intelligence. The prominence and widespread adoption of automated negotiation techniques have attracted much attention from researchers in multiple areas. Those areas include agreement technology, mechanism design, electronic commerce, recommender systems, supply chain management, and social choice theory. The ACAN series of workshops were created to disseminate findings and foster collaboration inside the community. The 13th international workshop on Agent-based Complex Automated Negotiations (ACAN 2022) was held in conjunction with the 31st International Joint Conference on Artificial Intelligence (IJCAI 2022). This book covers the selected papers presented at the 2022 ACAN workshop and the applications and challenges of agent-based negotiation. Top researchers in the field were invited to submit their recent findings. The Automated Negotiating Agent Competition (ANAC) is an important venue in the field of automated negotiation. We, therefore, invited the competition organizers to submit articles on their recent tournaments. All the invited papers will be reviewed by the editors. This book is intended for the academic and industrial researchers of various communities of autonomous agents and multi-agent systems, as well as graduate students studying in those areas or having an interest in them.

Book Organization

(A) Applications and Decision Support in Agent-Based Negotiation

(1) Marino Tejedor-Romero, Pradeep K. Murukannaiah, Jose Manuel Gimenez-Guzman, Ivan Marsa-Maestre, and Catholijn M. Jonker. "Distributed multi-agent negotiation for Wi-Fi channel assignment"

(2) Tomoki Kawazoe and Naoki Fukuta. "On Implementing a Simulation Environment for a Cooperative Multi-Agent Learning Approach to Mitigate DRDoS Attacks"

(3) Reyhan Aydoğan and Catholijn M. Jonker. "A Survey of Decision Support Mechanisms for Negotiation"

(4) Reyhan Aydoğan and Catholijn M. Jonker. "Bidding Support by the Pocket Negotiator Improves Negotiation Outcomes"

(B) Automated Negotiating Agent Competition

(1) Reyhan Aydoğan, Tim Baarslag, Katsuhide Fujita, Holger H. Hoos, Catholijn M. Jonker, Yasser Mohammad, and Bram M. Renting, "The 13th International Automated Negotiating Agent Competition Challenges and Results"

(2) Ahmet Burak Yildirim, Nezih Sunman, and Reyhan Aydoğan. "AhBuNe Agent: Winner of the Eleventh International Automated Negotiating Agent Competition (ANAC 2020)"

(3) Zongcan Li, Rafik Hadfi, and Takayuki Ito. "Agenda-based Automated Negotiation through Utility Decomposition"

(4) Yuchen Liu, Rafik Hadfi, and Takayuki Ito. "Concession Strategy Adjustment in Automated Negotiation Problems"

Keywords/Conference Topics

- Complex Automated Negotiations Frameworks and Mechanisms
- Bilateral and Multilateral Negotiations
- High Dimension Multi-Issue Negotiations
- Large-Scale Negotiations
- Concurrent Negotiations
- Multiple Negotiations
- Sequential Negotiations
- Negotiations under Asymmetric Information
- Prediction of Opponent's Behaviors and Strategies in Negotiations
- Machine Learning in Negotiations
- Simulation Models and Platforms for Complex Negotiations
- Coordination Mechanisms for Complex Negotiations
- Matchmaking and Brokering Mechanisms
- Utility and Preference Elicitation Technologies in Negotiations
- Utility and Preference Representations in Negotiations
- Computational Complexity of Multi-Issue Negotiations
- Negotiations with Humans, Negotiations in Social Networks, etc.
- Knowledge Management in Automated Negotiations.
- Moral consideration for automated negotiations.
- Real-life Aspects of Electronic Negotiations
- Applications for Automated Negotiations (e.g., cloud computing, smart grid, electronic commerce, etc.)

Contents

Contents

About the Editors

Dr. Rafik Hadfi is an assistant professor in the Department of Social Informatics at Kyoto University. His current research interests are designing, developing, and applying multi-agent systems to collective decision-making and social simulations. He is a recipient of the ANAC-IJCAI Supply Chain Management League Competition Award (2021), IBM Award of Scientific Excellence (2020), JSAI Annual Conference Award (2020), IPSJ Best Paper Award (2016), IEEE Young Researcher Award (2014), AAAI Student Scholarship Award (2014), and the Japanese Government MEXT Scholarship (2009). He serves as a program committee member in leading AI conferences such as IJCAI, AAMAS, and AAAI and is a reviewer for Artificial Intelligence Review, Neural Computation, Autonomous Agents and Multi-Agent Systems, and Group Decision and Negotiation. In addition, he has been the program chair, publication chair, workshop chair, tutorial chair, and volunteer chair for international AI conferences such as IEEE ICA, IJCAI, PRICAI, and PRIMA.

Dr. Reyhan Aydoğan is an assistant professor at Ozyegin University, Istanbul, and at the same time affiliated as a guest researcher in the Interactive Intelligence Group at the Delft University of Technology, the Netherlands. As a guest researcher, she visited the Center of Collective Intelligence at MIT in 2013, the Intelligence Systems Group at the Norwegian University of Science and Technology in 2015, and the Frontier Research Institute for Information Science at Nagoya Institute of Technology in 2017. Her research focuses on modeling, developing, and analyzing agent technologies that integrate different aspects of intelligence, such as reasoning, decision-making, and learning. She applies artificial intelligence techniques such as machine learning and semantic reasoning in designing and developing agent-based decision support systems, particularly negotiation support systems and automated negotiation tools. Dr. Aydoğan is one of the main organizers of the International Automated Negotiating Agents Competition (ANAC). She co-organized the following workshops: Conflict Resolution in Decision Making Workshop (COREDEMA) and International Workshop on Agent-based Complex Automated Negotiations (ACAN). She serves as a program committee member in reputable conferences such as AAAI, AAMAS, IJCAI, and ECAI. She served as a guest editor for the Special Issue on Artificial Intelligence Techniques for Conflict Resolution in Group Decision and Negotiation. Furthermore, she co-organized the 24th International Conference on Principles and Practice of Multi-agent Systems in 2022.

Dr. Takayuki Ito is a professor at Kyoto University. He received a B.E., M.E, and Doctor of Engineering from the Nagoya Institute of Technology in 1995, 1997, and 2000, respectively. From 1999 to 2001, he was a research fellow of the Japan Society for the Promotion of Science (JSPS). From 2000 to 2001, he was a visiting researcher at USC/ISI (University of Southern California/Information Sciences Institute). From April 2001 to March 2003, he was an associate professor at the Japan Advanced Institute of

Science and Technology (JAIST). From April 2004 to March 2013, he was an associate professor at the Nagoya Institute of Technology. From April 2014 to September 2020, he was a professor at the Nagoya Institute of Technology. In October 2020, he joined Kyoto University. From 2005 to 2006, he was a visiting researcher at the Division of Engineering and Applied Science, Harvard University, and a visiting researcher at the Center for Coordination Science, MIT Sloan School of Management. From 2008 to 2010, he was a visiting researcher at the Center for Collective Intelligence, MIT Sloan School of Management. From 2017 to 2018, he is an invited researcher of the Artificial Intelligence Center of AIST, Japan. Since March 5, 2019, he is the CTO of AgreeBit, inc. He is a board member of IFAAMAS, an executive committee member of the IEEE Computer Society Technical Committee on Intelligent Informatics, the PC chair of AAMAS2013, PRIMA2009, the local arrangements chair of IJCAI-PRICAI2020, the general chair of PRIMA2014, and was an SPC/PC member in many top-level conferences (IJCAI, AAMAS, ECAI, AAAI, etc.). He received the Japan Society for Artificial Intelligence (JSAI) Contribution Award, the JSAI Achievement Award, the JSPS Prize, 2014, the Prize for Science and Technology (Research Category), The Commendation for Science and Technology by the Minister of Education, Culture, Sports, Science, and Technology, 2013, the Young Scientists' Prize, The Commendation for Science and Technology by the Minister of Education, Culture, Sports, Science, and Technology, 2007, the Nagao Special Research Award of the Information Processing Society of Japan, 2007, the Best Paper Award of AAMAS2006, the 2005 Best Paper Award from Japan Society for Software Science and Technology, the Best Paper Award in the 66th annual conference of 66th Information Processing Society of Japan, and the Super Creator Award of 2004 IPA Exploratory Software Creation Projects. He is the principal investigator of the Japan Cabinet Funding Program for Next Generation World-Leading Researchers (NEXT Program). Further, he has several companies handling web-based and enterprise-distributed systems. His main research interests include multi-agent systems, intelligent agents, collective intelligence, group decision support system, etc.

Dr. Ryuta Arisaka is an assistant professor at Kyoto University. His interests cover mathematical and philosophical logic, formal and informal argumentation, and formal methods in program analysis. He obtained BSc in Computer Science (1st Hons, 83% average in final years exams) and MPhil in Computer Science from the University of Manchester, UK, and subsequently, a Ph.D. in Computer Science, also in the UK. He conducted research on mathematical logic and formal argumentation at Inria-Saclay (Palaiseau, France), National Institute of Informatics (Tokyo, Japan), Perugia University (Perugia, Italy), and Nagoya Institute of Technology (Nagoya, Japan), before joining Kyoto University. He was awarded the Best Paper Award for his research on formal argumentation semantics at PRICAI 2019 and argumentation-based multi-agent concurrent negotiations at ACAN 2019. He was a program co-chair of IEEE ICA2021. He has served as a program committee member of AAAI, IJCAI, PRIMA, and other international workshops.

Applications and Decision Support in Agent-Based Negotiation

Distributed Multi-agent Negotiation for Wi-Fi Channel Assignment

Marino Tejedor-Romero[1][✉] ⓘ, Pradeep K. Murukannaiah[2] ⓘ,
Jose Manuel Gimenez-Guzman[3] ⓘ, Ivan Marsa-Maestre[1] ⓘ,
and Catholijn M. Jonker[2] ⓘ

[1] University of Alcala, Alcala de Henares, Spain
{marino.tejedor,ivan.marsa}@uah.es
[2] Technical University of Delft, Delft, The Netherlands
{P.K.Murukannaiah,C.M.Jonker}@tudelft.nl
[3] Universitat Politècnica de València, València, Spain
jmgimenez@upv.es

Abstract. Channel allocation in dense, decentralized Wi-Fi networks
is a challenging due to the highly nonlinear solution space and the difficulty to estimate the opponent's utility model. So far, only centralized or
mediated approaches have succeeded in applying negotiation to this setting. We propose the first two fully-distributed negotiation approaches
for Wi-Fi channel assignment. Both of them leverage a pre-sampling
of the utility space with simulated annealing and a noisy estimation of
the Wi-Fi utility function. Regarding negotiation protocols, one of the
approaches makes use of the Alternating Offers protocol, while the other
uses the novel Multiple Offers Protocol for Multilateral Negotiations with
Partial Consensus (MOPaC), which naturally matches the problem peculiarities. We compare the performance of our proposed approaches with
the previous mediated approach, based on simple text mediation. Our
experiments show that our approaches yield better utility outcomes, better fairness and less information disclosure than the mediated approach.

Keywords: Wi-Fi networks · Simulated annealing · Automated
negotiation

1 Introduction

Automated negotiation enables efficient distributed solutions for problems which
are distributed by nature, but that due to their complexity tend to end up
resorting to centralized management. A paradigmatic example of such a problem
is Wi-Fi channel assignment. The *de facto* standard for dense, uncoordinated
Wi-Fi networks is distributed [1], but it usually yields suboptimal allocations.
Due to this, most managed settings resort to centralized solutions, which often
disregard individual utilities in the search for a global optimum.

© The Author(s), under exclusive license to Springer Nature Singapore Pte Ltd. 2023
R. Hadfi et al. (Eds.): IJCAI 2022, SCI 1092, pp. 3–14, 2023.
https://doi.org/10.1007/978-981-99-0561-4_1

In previous work, we proposed Wi-Fi channel assignment as a realistic and challenging benchmark for complex automated negotiations [2,6,11]. In this setting, different Wi-Fi providers, acting as agents, collectively decide how to distribute the channels used by their access points (APs) to minimize interference between nodes and maximize utility (i.e., network throughput) for their clients, which are different kinds of wireless devices, usually called stations (STAs).

We proposed a number of approaches in the Wi-Fi negotiation setting. However, the complexity of the negotiation domain, along with the difficulty to estimate utility *a priori*, forced us to resort to mediated settings. The most successful approach was based on simple text mediation and simulated annealing [11]. Although the approach clearly outperformed the *de facto* standard, it required a large number of bidding rounds by the agents (on the order of thousands), apart from raising great concerns in terms of communication efficiency and privacy.

In this work, we propose novel distributed negotiation approaches intended for Wi-Fi channel assignment. Further, we want to test the hypotheses that these approaches can be used as an efficient alternative to the centralized ones. This work contributes to achieve this goal in the following ways:

- We describe the Wi-Fi channel assignment as a negotiation problem, and our previous mediated approach (Sect. 2).
- We propose a pre-sampling of the utility space with simulated annealing and a noisy estimation of the Wi-Fi utility function. Then, we incorporate these techniques to two negotiation protocols: Alternating Offers and Multilateral Negotiations with Partial Consensus (MOPaC) (Sect. 3).
- We validate our approaches on a real-world setting modelling a residential building, comparing our negotiation approaches to two reference techniques: the *de facto* standard in Wi-Fi networks based on choosing the least congested channel and our previous work of centralized mediation (Sect. 4).

The experimental results (Sect. 4.3) show that our benchmarked negotiation approaches significantly outperform the *de facto* standard and the centralized mediator in terms of social welfare and Nash product. In addition, we observe better fairness results with the distributed approaches, and a clear advantage in terms of communication efficiency and privacy. The last section includes a summary, concluding remark, and directions.

2 Wi-Fi Channel Assignment: A Challenging Negotiation Domain

We briefly review the previous work on applying negotiation to Wi-Fi channel assignment. First we discuss the peculiarities of the problem and the notion of utility we use (which is based on Wi-Fi throughput), and then we describe the mediated negotiation approach we will compare our proposals with.

2.1   Wi-Fi Performance and Utility

IEEE 802.11 based networks, commercially known as Wi-Fi networks, have greatly changed the way users connect to Internet, mainly due to their infrastructure mode operation. In this mode, Wi-Fi networks are made up of two types of devices: access points (APs) and stations (STAs). More specifically, in infrastructure-mode Wi-Fi networks, each STA is associated with an AP, so that each STA can only communicate directly with its AP, so if two STAs want to communicate, they must communicate by means of, at least, an AP.

One of the reasons for the great popularity of Wi-Fi networks is that they are deployed in unlicensed frequency bands, so anyone can use these bands freely. The most popular examples of unlicensed frequency bands where Wi-Fi networks operate in are the so-called 2.4 GHz and 5 GHz frequency bands. Although our work can be easily extrapolated to the 5 GHz frequency band, we focus on the 2.4 GHz one as it is still the most widely used and congested, so it is the one where our proposal can become more advantageous. We consider the standard IEEE 802.11n (Wi-Fi 4) operating in the 2.4 GHz band. In this context, there are 11 possible channels in which each AP (and, therefore, all their associated STAs) can operate. These 11 channels are not orthogonal, but partially collide, which makes the problem of channel assignment even more challenging.

To study the problem of Wi-Fi channel assignment, we have modeled Wi-Fi networks by means of geometric 3D graphs. Graphs let us to accurately describe the network behavior while keeping the model abstract and reusable. Formally, a graph can be defined as a set of vertices (V) and a set of edges (E) connecting those vertices, $E \subseteq \{(u,v) \mid u, v \in V\}$. This geometric graph has two types of vertices (APs and STAs) and two types of edges—one represents the interfering signals, and the other represents the desired signal between each STA and its associated AP. As a consequence, and using a specific propagation model (we have used the indoor propagation model proposed by ITU-R in the Recommendation P-1230-10), for each STA, the graph model yields not only the power of the signal an STA receives from its AP, but also the power of all the interferences that are received by that STA. Therefore, the graph model will let us to compute the Signal-to-Interference-plus-Noise Ratio (SINR), computed as the quotient between the power of the received signal from the AP divided by the sum of the powers of all the interferences plus the thermal noise. SINR is a key performance parameter that defines the throughput, which is the main performance parameter that defines the quality of service perceived by the final user. In this sense, depending on the SINR a certain MCS (Modulation and Coding Scheme) can be used, as defined in the Wi-Fi 4 standard. For example, as the SINR grows, we will be able to use coding schemes with less redundancy together with digital modulations with a higher number of bits per symbol.

The utility function we use for the negotiation is based on the throughput model for each AP and STA, depending on the chosen channels. The problem settings (high cardinality of the solution space and attribute interdependence) make the utility functions highly complex, with multiple local optima.

2.2   Mediated Negotiation for Wi-Fi Channel Assignment

Given the above discussion, we formally define different elements of the problem. For a channel assignment problem with n_{AP} access points, P is the set of access points. A solution or deal $S = (s_1, s_2, s_3, \ldots, s_{n_{AP}})$, where each $s_i \in \{1, \ldots, 11\}$, represents the assignation of a Wi-Fi channel to the i-th access point.

We assume that there are different network providers (commonly Internet Service Providers, ISPs) or agents. Thus, APs belong to one of the agents. Each provider only has control over the channel assignment for its own access points. According to this situation, the agents will negotiate the channel assignment. Finally, each one of these agents will compute its utility for a certain solution according to the model described in the previous section.

$A = \{1, 2, \ldots, n_a\}$ is the set containing every agent in the channel assignment problem. The set P is partitioned into n_a subsets, one for each agent. P_a is the subset of access points which belong to agent a.

The utility of an agent depends on the throughput estimated for each solution S. Our model returns the estimated throughput of each access point for the given vector of channels. The global utility for a solution S is U_S and can be calculated as the sum of all throughput values. However, it is more important to define agent-dependant utilities. The utility obtained by agent a for a solution S, $u_{S,a}$, is the sum of the throughput values of the corresponding access points, i.e., the sum of the throughput values for the access points in P_a. The opponent utility, $u_{S,a}^c$, is the sum of the throughput of every access point which does not belong to a, i.e., the sum of the throughput values for the access points in $P - P_a$. Further, for protocols requiring a normalized utility in $[0, 1]$, we can divide the utility by the maximum ideal throughput obtained with no interference whatsoever.

In our previous work on this setting [2,6,11], we used several variations of the simple text mediation protocol [9]. The most successful technique after our previous experiments worked as follows:

1. The mediator starts with a randomly-generated candidate contract (S_0^c). This means to assign each AP a random channel.
2. In each iteration t, the mediator proposes a contract S_t^c to the rest of agents. To generate the next candidate contract S_t^c, the mediator takes the base contract S_{t-1}^c and mutates one of its issues randomly. This corresponds to choosing a random access point and selecting a new random channel for it.
3. Each agent either accepts or rejects the contract S_t^c. To perform this decision, we use a widespread nonlinear optimization technique called simulated annealing (SA) [8]. With this technique, when a contract yields a utility loss against the previous mutually accepted contract, there will be a probability for the agent to accept it nonetheless. This probability depends on the utility loss Δu associated to the new contract and *annealing temperature* τ, and is equal to $e^{\frac{-\Delta u}{\tau}}$. Annealing temperature begins at an initial value, and linearly decreases over the successive iterations of the protocol.
4. The mediator generates a new contract S_{t+1}^c from the previous contracts and from the votes received from the agents. At time t, if all agents have accepted

the presented contract S_t^c, this contract will be used as the base contract S^b to generate the next contract S_{t+1}^c. Otherwise, the last mutually accepted contract will be used. The process moves to step 2.

5. After a fixed number of iterations, the mediator advertises the last mutually accepted contract as final.

Although the negotiation mechanism above yielded satisfactory results in terms of social welfare, it had a number of limitations. First, since it optimized the sum of utilities, it had a tendency to produce unfair assignments. Second, it needed the agents to vote over thousands of contracts during the negotiation, which involved a significant communication overhead and a potential privacy concern. Our hypothesis is that these limitations can be overcome by using distributed, unmediated negotiation approaches, which we propose next.

3   Unmediated Techniques for Wi-Fi Channel Negotiation

We propose novel approaches for Wi-Fi negotiation. To our knowledge, these are first unmediated negotiation approaches succeeding in this setting.

Our aim is to apply state-of-the art negotiation techniques to the Wi-Fi domain, in order to benefit from the variety of approaches in the literature. However, the peculiarities of the setting prevent the application of most of these techniques. One of the main obstacles is the unfeasibility of performing an exhaustive search over the utility space, due to high cardinality. For instance, in the scenario analyzed in the validation, the number of bids is 11^{40}. Many negotiation approaches, such as the ones implemented in GENIUS [5], rely on the agent having an ordered set of bids, so that it may choose at each step in the negotiation an adequate bid according to the agent's current aspirational level. The other main challenge is how to obtain bids that correspond to "good negotiation moves," and it is related to negotiation predictability. Being able to (partly) predict the preference profile of the other negotiators makes it easier to make an offer that the other party can accept, and increases the possibility of reaching a good negotiation outcome more quickly [12]. This is specially challenging in our scenario for two reasons. First, the utility spaces are highly rugged, so linearity, concavity or convexity assumptions are not possible. Second, the utility for the agents depend on the precise location of APs and STAs at a given time, which may not be known with full precision. Therefore, there is an uncertainty not only about the opponent's utility function, but also about the agent's one.

In the following, we describe the techniques used to overcome these two challenges, and then the protocols used for the negotiation.

3.1   Estimating Utility Through the Graph Model

Although estimating the opponent utility is challenging for the Wi-Fi channel negotiation domain, we need these values for the negotiation. To address this challenge, we rely on the graph model.

We assume that each agent knows the position of their access points, and the position of every client connected to those access points. However, this is not enough to obtain the estimated throughput. We must know the position of all the devices in the Wi-Fi network. For this purpose, agents can use Wi-Fi localization techniques. The state-of-the-art approaches such as [4,10] allow positioning these devices with an error below 1.7 m. Thus, it is realistic to assume that every agent can have their own estimated version of the Wi-Fi graph. Its own access points and devices will have accurate positions, while the rest of the devices have an approximate position. In our benchmarks, we simulate this behaviour, adding a Gaussian noise to the position of the unknown devices. In particular, we add a random distance determined by a Gaussian distribution with $\sigma = 1.7$ in a random direction, following the results described in [4,10].

3.2 Annealing Exploration

To allow agents to have a tractable, ordered set of bids to use in the negotiation, we leverage the success of the previous approach in making an efficient exploration of the utility space in the search for an optimum. Since the annealer optimizer used in [2,6,11] was able to "climb" the utility space from a random contract to an optimum, we are going to use the same approach at each agent individually, to come up with a small subset of bids covering a wide variety of utility values for the agent. The process works similarly as the one described in Sect. 2.2, with a number of minor adjustments due to the fact that now it is an individual process performed at every agent prior to the negotiation:

1. Each agent a starts with a randomly-generated candidate bid $(S_{0,a})$.
2. In each iteration t, the agent generates a simple mutation of the bid $S_{t,a}$, changing only one of the issues to a random value.
3. The agent calculates the utility of the new candidate bid for itself $(u_{S_t,a})$, which depends on the resulting throughput of its access points, and the opponent's utility (u_{t,a^c}), which depends on the resulting throughput of every other access point that does not belong to agent a.
4. This bid $(S_{t,a})$, its own utility $(u_{S_t,a})$ and the opponent's utility $(u^c_{S_t,a})$ are stored.
5. The agent chooses whether to use the candidate bid $S_{t,a}$ as the base bid to generate the next bid $S_{t+1,a}$ or to maintain the previous base bid. This is done by annealing, with a probability depending on the utility loss for the agent associated to the new bid $\Delta u_a = u_{S_t,a} - u_{S_{t-1},a}$ and the *annealing temperature* τ, as described above. The process moves to step 2.
6. After a fixed number of iterations, the agent stops exploring and obtains a set of bids with associated utilities for itself and for the opponents.

At the end of this process, each agent will have sampled its bid space in a directed way, to maximize its utility. Since we store all the history of the annealer exploration process, along with the utility for each bid, we have an ordered subset of the bid space covering a variety of aspiration levels for the agent. This can be used to apply conventional negotiation strategies to this new setting.

3.3   SAOP-Based Unmediated Negotiation

Without a mediator, it is necessary to follow an automated negotiation protocol. Simple Alternating Offering Protocol (SAOP) is a clear example [3]. In SAOP, for each round of negotiation, one of the agents offers a contract, and the other evaluates it, accepting it or not depending on its utility. In the next round, they reverse their roles. The negotiation continues until a contract is accepted.

In order to test our annealing exploration of the contract space and our opponent's utility estimation method, we created a new agent for the SAOP protocol, designed to negotiate on the Wi-Fi channel domain, in a bilateral setting. Our agent's bidding strategy is inspired by time-dependent agents. Time-dependent agents start proposing the bid which yields maximum utility for them, but they make concessions throughout the negotiation rounds, lowering their utility goals. Each agent proceeds as follows:

1. The agent runs one or several simulated annealers, aiming to maximize their own function, according to the technique explained in Sect. 3.2. This is a preparation stage, prior to any communication between agents.
2. Every round, the agent calculates its utility goal. Since the negotiation takes place in a fixed number of rounds, the typical behavior is to start aiming for the maximum utility, lowering the goal as the negotiation advances, in order to achieve an agreement. The utility goal function can be configured, following different strategies, but for simplicity, we are using linear concession.
   - If it is the agent's turn to offer a contract, it extracts the subset of contracts that satisfy the goal. For this subset, it sends the contract with the greater estimated utility for the rest of the agents.
   - On the contrary, if the agent evaluates an incoming offer, it simply checks if the received contract satisfies the goal.

3.4   MOPaC-Based Unmediated Negotiation

Our previous working strategy, mediated negotiation based on simulated annealing, can be generalized to any number of network providers or agents. However, the agent we designed for SAOP works only for bilateral negotiation. To generalize unmediated negotiation for multiple agents, we choose a different protocol that supports multi-party negotiations and enables us to adapt our agent.

We choose the Multiple Offers Protocol for Multilateral Negotiations with Partial Consensus (MOPaC) [13]. In MOPaC, at the beginning of a round, every agent proposes a contract to a common pool. Then, every agent evaluates every contract in the pool, communicating if the vote is positive or negative, and a minimum and maximum consensus threshold. This protocol does not require a full consensus, and can be configured to search for multiple partial consensus.

The first two steps are similar: the agent runs one or several explorations through simulated annealing. Then, for each round, the agent calculates its utility goal, using any configured progression function, linear or not. The biding behavior is also similar: given a utility goal, the agent extracts a subset of contracts which satisfy this goal, and send the one that yields more opponent utility.

In a multi-party negotiation, there is one utility for each opponent. As a last step, in the voting phase, agents vote using their utility goal, looking for consensus.

While MOPaC allows partial consensus, we are, for the moment, forcing a complete agreement. The possibility of reaching several partial agreements can make our approach richer and more versatile, but we are still exploring this idea, as we will cover in the Future Work section.

4   Experimental Evaluation

4.1   Considered Scenario

We conduct our experiments in a realistic scenario that models a 5-floor residential building as a paradigmatic example where multiple Wi-Fi networks coexist. In this setting, each floor has a length, width and height of 40, 30 and 3 m, and there are eight flats in each floor in a 4×2 layout. In each flat, there is one AP and four STAs. Every STA in a flat is associated to the AP from the same flat, even when there are closer APs from contiguous flats. For each flat, the position of the AP and its STAs follows a uniform distribution in the x- and y-axis, but, in the z-axis, the position of each AP and STA is normally distributed in each floor with a mean of 1.5 m and a standard deviation of 0.5 m, being this random height also bounded to the limits of the floor. In summary, our experimental setting consists of 40 APs distributed along 5 floors and 40×4 = 160 $STAs$, where there are 4 STAs associated to each AP. Figure 1 shows a graphical representation of the experimental layout under study.

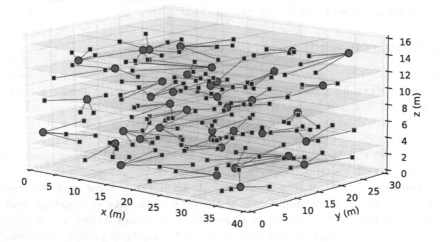

Fig. 1. Considered scenario for experimental evaluation.

4.2   Experimental Settings

The techniques used for evaluation have been described above, but we summarize them here for convenience.

- *Least Congested Channel search (LCCS)*: LCCS is the de facto standard for Wi-Fi channel assignment [1]. It is based on each AP sensing the channel occupation and asynchronously choosing the channel where it finds the lowest interferences from other active APs and their clients. We implemented a coordinated LCCS, where there is a centralized controller which evaluates the proposed changes before actually implementing them, thus preventing utility oscillations. This is a usual implementation in corporate environments.
- *Mediated negotiation with two and four agents (MN-2 and MN-4)*: The mediated approach we used in our previous works [2,6,11], which we described in Sect. 2.2. To allow for a better comparison with the two approaches we propose, we run experiments with two and four agents.
- *Annealer exploration and alternating offers protocol (AE-AOP)*: Here, we perform the initial exploration of the agent utility spaces described in Sect. 3.2, and then we use a bilateral SAOP (Sect. 3.3) for the negotiation.
- *Annealer exploration and MOPaC (AE-MOPaC)*: Again, we perform the initial exploration of the agent utility spaces described in Sect. 3.2, but then we use MOPaC (Sect. 3.4) with four agents for the negotiation.

In all cases, the distribution of APs among the different agents was performed randomly for each trial. Agent utility functions were generated making noisy estimations of the real Wi-Fi graph as described in Sect. 3.1. Again, these estimations were generated randomly for each agent and trial.

Each technique was run for 100 times over the scenario described above. For each run, we measured social welfare, the Nash product, and the Jain index for fairness [7], which is widely used in the wireless network domain. These metrics will be briefly described in the next section.

4.3   Experimental Results

Table 1 summarizes our results. The first measure we can compare is social welfare, measured globally in Mbit/s. It is the sum of the complete throughput vector. LCCS, the de facto standard, obtains the lowest social welfare. The two highest values are from AE-MOPaC, and AE-AOP, which are based on unmediated negotiations with two and four agents, respectively. The corresponding mediated counterparts with two and four agents offer a better social welfare compared to LCCS. However, note that the unmediated negotiation scores higher than the mediated negotiation if we maintain the number of agents; that is, AE-AOP improves MN-2 result and AE-MOPaC improves MN-4 result.

The Nash product and fairness index cannot be compared globally. The Nash product can be compared only between techniques with the same number of agents. In this comparison, the unmediated negotiations obtain approximately 1.5 times the Nash product of the mediated counterpart, which is an important

Table 1. Comparing the proposed decentralized approaches (AE-MOPaC, and AE-AOP) with mediated approaches (MN-2 and MN-4) and the de facto standard (LCCS). Average values (avg) and confidence intervals (CI) are reported.

	Social Welfare		Nash Product		Jain's Fairness		Comm. Overhead
	Avg	CI	Avg	CI	Avg	CI	Avg
LCCS	626.66	9.29	–		–		0
MN-2	637.39	10.88	$9.54 \cdot 10^4$	$3.40 \cdot 10^3$	0.938	0.007	$3 \cdot 10^3$
AE-AOP	787.54	8.85	$1.50 \cdot 10^5$	$3.31 \cdot 10^3$	0.967	0.004	$5 \cdot 10^1$
MN-4	760.24	15.52	$1.08 \cdot 10^9$	$8.80 \cdot 10^7$	0.907	0.011	$3 \cdot 10^3$
AE-MOPaC	817.57	12.85	$1.58 \cdot 10^9$	$1.05 \cdot 10^8$	0.949	0.014	$5 \cdot 10^1$

improvement. Fairness can be compared only between negotiation techniques, leaving LCCS outside of the comparison. Again, it is only fair to compare negotiations with similar number of agents. In this case, we can perceive significant improvements in the fairness of the results using unmediated negotiation over mediated counterparts, although the improvement is more modest.

The communication overhead depends on the protocol. LCCS requires no communication between access points, making it the most simple and lightweight approach. Mediated negotiation requires a number of messages equal to the number of contracts proposed in the simulated annealing process. In our experiments, the communication overhead is 3000 interactions, since we have used 3000 iterations for all the simulated annealing executions. In the unmediated negotiations, agents run their annealing exploration processes independently, eliminating the overhead of 3000 iterations. However, they still need to propose contracts until one of them is accepted. In other words, the communication overhead depends on the negotiation rounds. This parameter is configurable, and we used 50 rounds for our experiments. This is an upper bound, since the actual number of rounds is mostly below 50 rounds, before it reaches the deadline.

5   Conclusions and Future Work

Optimizing the performance of Wi-Fi networks through channel assignment is an example of a distributed critical real-world problem. In the past, we addressed this challenge using mediated negotiation. This paper aims to advance towards a more distributed solution, evaluating the use of fully unmediated negotiation techniques. We compare the negotiation-based approaches with both the *de facto* standard for Wi-Fi channel assignment and our previous mediated approach. Our current experiments show an improvement of performance over the mediated approach in terms of social welfare, Nash product, and fairness.

This paper opens several research directions. First of all, it is important to optimize simulated annealing parameters so we can properly compare the optimal performance of unmediated and mediated negotiation techniques. Another open challenge of our approach is how to use opponent's offers to refine our utility model throughout the negotiation. Finally, we would want to explore other strategies and partial consensus formation approaches for MOPaC.

Acknowledgement. Marino Tejedor Romero, Jose Manuel Gimenez-Guzman and Ivan Marsa-Maestre are supported by Project SBPLY/19/180501/000171 of the Junta de Comunidades de Castilla-La Mancha and FEDER, by Project UCeNet (CM/JIN/2019-031) of the Comunidad de Madrid and University of Alcalá, and by Project PID2019-104855RB-I00/AEI/10.13039/501100011033 of the Spanish Ministry of Science and Innovation. Marino Tejedor Romero and Ivan Marsa-Maestre are supported by Project WiDAI (CM/JIN/2021-004) of the Comunidad de Madrid and University of Alcalá. Marino Tejedor is also funded by a predoctoral contract from University of Alcalá.

References

1. Achanta, M.: Method and apparatus for least congested channel scan for wireless access points. US Patent App. 10/959,446. 6 Apr 2006
2. De La Hoz, E., Marsa-Maestre, I., Gimenez-Guzman, J.M., Orden, D., Klein, M.: Multi-agent nonlinear negotiation for Wi-Fi channel assignment. In: Proceedings of the 16th Conference on Autonomous Agents and MultiAgent Systems, pp. 1035–1043. International Foundation for Autonomous Agents and Multiagent Systems (2017)
3. Fatima, S., Kraus, S., Wooldridge, M.: Principles of Automated Negotiation: Cambridge University Press, Cambridge (October 2014)
4. Han, K., Yu, S.M., Kim, S.L., Ko, S.W.: Exploiting user mobility for WIFI RTT positioning: a geometric approach. IEEE Internet Things J. **8**(19), 14589–14606 (2021)
5. Hindriks, K., Jonker, C.M., Kraus, S., Lin, R., Tykhonov, D.: Genius: negotiation environment for heterogeneous agents. In: Proceedings of the 8th International Conference on Autonomous Agents and Multiagent Systems-Volume 2. pp. 1397–1398 (2009)
6. de la Hoz, E., Gimenez-Guzman, J.M., Marsa-Maestre, I., Orden, D.: Automated negotiation for resource assignment in wireless surveillance sensor networks. Sensors **15**(11), 29547–29568 (2015)
7. Jain, R.K., Chiu, D.M.W., Hawe, W.R., et al.: A Quantitative Measure of Fairness and Discrimination. Eastern Research Laboratory, Digital Equipment Corporation, Hudson, MA 21 (1984)
8. Kirkpatrick, S., Gelatt, C.D., Vecchi, M.P.: Optimization by simulated annealing. Science **220**(4598), 671 (1983). https://doi.org/10.1126/science.220.4598.671
9. Klein, M., Faratin, P., Sayama, H., Bar-Yam, Y.: Negotiating complex contracts. Group Decis. Negot. **12**(2), 111–125 (2003). https://doi.org/10.1023/A:1023068821218
10. Li, S., Hedley, M., Bengston, K., Humphrey, D., Johnson, M., Ni, W.: Passive localization of standard WIFI devices. IEEE Syst. J. **13**(4), 3929–3932 (2019)
11. Marsa-Maestre, I., de la Hoz, E., Gimenez-Guzman, J.M., Orden, D., Klein, M.: Nonlinear negotiation approaches for complex-network optimization: a study inspired by WI-FI channel assignment. Group Decis. Negot. **28**(1), 175–196 (2019)

12. Marsa-Maestre, I., Klein, M., Jonker, C.M., Aydoğan, R.: From problems to protocols: towards a negotiation handbook. Decis. Support Syst. **60**, 39–54 (2014)
13. Murukannaiah, P.K., Jonker, C.M.: MOPaC: the multiple offers protocol for multilateral negotiations with partial consensus (2022). https://doi.org/10.48550/ARXIV.2205.06678, https://arxiv.org/abs/2205.06678

On Implementing a Simulation Environment for a Cooperative Multi-agent Learning Approach to Mitigate DRDoS Attacks

Tomoki Kawazoe[1]([✉]) and Naoki Fukuta[2][iD]

[1] Shizuoka University, Shizuoka, Japan
kawazoe.tomoki.17@shizuoka.ac.jp
[2] Shizuoka University, Shizuoka, Japan
fukuta@inf.shizuoka.ac.jp

Abstract. One of serious threats on the Internet is a Distributed Reflective Denial-of-Service (DRDoS) attack. We are aiming to realize defenders that can deal with more sophisticated cooperative and strategic attacks which are becoming realistic and will be seen in the future. Specifically, we focus on an environment where there are attackers that can change their strategy of the DRDoS attacks in consideration of the alliance among the defenders, which we will require to develop the defenders which can give misleading information to fool the attackers about the recognition of alliance state and to coordinate their filtering strategy so that they utilize the current alliance among the defenders with maximum efficiency of the throughput for ordinary traffics. For achieving the final goal, we consider the simulation method of the DRDoS attacks including the attackers and the defenders that can respond dynamically according to the environment, and consider the method for building the environment. In our work, we also consider the DRDoS attackers that dynamically change their behavior, a method for a simulation in order to proceed the defenders' Multi-Agent Reinforcement Learning (MARL) in an environment where there are the defenders against the attackers, the environment, and a MARL method to be applied there.

Keywords: Multi-agent learning · Security · DRDoS

1 Introduction

As the Internet is expanding and becoming the part of social infrastructure, the security threats compromising the availability of software and services utilized via the network are a serious problem. One of these serious threats is a Denial of Service (DoS) attack. When the DoS attacks are carried out in distributed form using botnets, the attack is called Distributed DoS (DDoS) attack [7]. Furthermore, when the attackers exploit legitimate servers with requests with the victim's spoofed source address, and causes the servers to return an attack

© The Author(s), under exclusive license to Springer Nature Singapore Pte Ltd. 2023
R. Hadfi et al. (Eds.): IJCAI 2022, SCI 1092, pp. 15–29, 2023.
https://doi.org/10.1007/978-981-99-0561-4_2

response to the victim, the attack is called a "Distributed Reflective Denial-of-Service (DRDoS)" attack [9]. In many cases, the responses generated by the servers are amplified compared to the requests sent by the attacker. Therefore, a DRDoS attack is also called "amplified DDoS" attack [4].

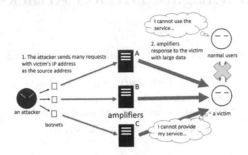

Fig. 1. A brief example of DRDoS. At first, many botnets send many requests with the victim's IP address as the source address. Then, the amplifiers respond to the victim with large data.

Figure 1 shows a brief example of the behavior of DRDoS attacks. The DRDoS attacks amplify many small requests sent by the attackers exploiting many servers or systems that is open to the public whether intentionally or not, normally the amplification rate is 10–500× [9], and then induce the exhaustion the network resource such as the bandwidth and computation resource of the target victim.

1.1 Attackers Assumed in This Research

Several approaches have been proposed to detect DRDoS attacks [2,12]. Shurman et al. proposed a deep learning model based on LSTM, able to detect DRDoS attacks [12]. It was trained and evaluated on CICDDoS2019 dataset [10] which is contained two kinds of DRDoS attacks, and the proposed model shows an accuracy higher than 99%. The dataset CICDDoS2019 used in the research is producing realistic DDoS attack dataset including DRDoS attacks [10]. Furthermore, there were some approaches such as some methods in which some Internet Exchange Points (IXPs) cooperate [14] and some Internet Service Providers (ISPs) cooperate for mitigating DRDoS attacks [6].

Although numerous mitigation methods for the DDoS attacks and the DRDoS attacks have been proposed [5,8,14,16], the frequency and intensity of DDoS attacks still continue to grow without signs of stopping [7]. In addition, there are some attackers which make no-constant pulsed attacks to maximize the attacking efficiency, minimize the attacking cost, and continue to exploit the vulnerable servers used as amplifier (amp server) without going down [4]. Based on these survey results, it may be needed to think about the attackers that perform more sophisticated attacks, and to deal with such attackers.

In this research, we assume that the attackers can dynamically change its behavior in consideration of the environment including the alliance among defenders. This means the attackers can launch DRDoS attacks that nullify the conventional defense methods.

1.2   Assumed Approach to Overcome the Strategic Attacks

We aim to realize defenders which can deal with such attackers mentioned above. We assume that where there are attackers which change their strategy of the DRDoS attacks in consideration of the alliance among the defenders. To fight against this situation, we need to develop the defenders which give misleading information to fool the attackers about the alliance among defenders while also giving the possible maximum efficiency of throughputs. In this decision-making process for the defenders, it is necessary for the defenders to dynamically make the decision or negotiate in consideration of other defenders according to the environment. For this reason, we are seeking an idea of employing "Multi-Agent Reinforcement Learning (MARL)" to implement cooperative defenders.

1.3   The Aim

To achieve our final goal, we first aim to develop a simulation method of DRDoS attacks including the attackers and the defenders which can respond dynamically according to the environment, and consider the method for building the environment. We aim to prepare a way to reproduce the DRDoS attackers which dynamically change their behavior, simulator in order to execute the learning process of defenders' MARL in an environment where there are the defenders against the attackers, and the environment.

2   Modeling DRDoS

2.1   Overview of DRDoS Attacks

The purpose of DRDoS attacks is causing the congestion of victim's bandwidth by sending numerous traffic toward a victim, and then disabling the victim's service. To this end, attackers use many amplifiers. The amplifiers are machine or service that is open access and usually return 10-500x response to a specific request [9]. Therefore, the amplifier is called "reflector". The attackers send many requests with the victim's IP address as the source address, and then the amplifiers return many amplified responses toward the victim. The brief overview of this attack is shown in Fig. 1.

Here, we can notice the fact that there are two types of attack flow in DRDoS attacks. One shows spoofed requests sent by attackers toward vulnerable open access servers/services exploited as triggers of amplified responses. The other shows amplified responses sent by vulnerable amp servers toward a victim.

2.2   Modeling Attackers and Defenders

In this section, we show examples of attackers' response such as considered in current researches, and then explain examples of it considered in this research, finally explain examples of defenders' response corresponding to the attackers. Note that figures shown in this section do not include behavior of normal users, however it is important to consider the behavior of normal users since the pass rate of packets sent by normal users during DRDoS attacks is an evaluation indicator.

Figure 2, 3, 4, 5, and 6 show a set of examples to show the attackers' standard behaviors in DRDoS. After a state shown in Fig. 2, the state transitions to Fig. 3, 4, 5, or 6 depend on attackers' and defenders' strategies. Figure 2, 3, and 4 show how current DRDoS attacks will be done in an environment where there are defenders which cooperate with other ones and mitigate the attacks on the way of the attacks path. The attackers shown in Fig. 2, 3, and 4 will do attacks in a constant manner without taking into account alliance among defenders. In contrast to the attackers, Fig. 5 shows that the attackers can dynamically change their attacking strategies in consideration of the cooperative behavior of defenders that are on the way of the attack path. Their behavior indicated that they try to conduct their attacks at maximum efficiency in minimum cost. An example behavior of defenders which attempt to overcome the strategic attacks is shown in Fig. 6. Here, the defenders cooperate with "C" in addition to "A" and "B", and then switch to a strategy in which only "C" blocks the attacks when the attackers attempt to send more spoofed request packets to "C". This response maintains the availability of services provided by "A", "B", and "victim", and then the defenders can obtain maximum availability at minimum cost as a whole.

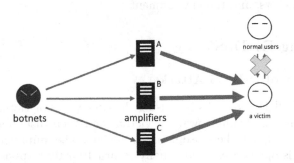

Fig. 2. This figure shows the situation that attackers are attacking the victim by exploiting some amplifier servers and the victim's service is down.

In this research, we assume that ISPs on the path of DRDoS attacks play the role of defenders for mitigating the attacks. These defenders regard the decision making in the environment where DRDoS attacks are performed as a Markov Decision Process, and then try to perform a multi-agent learning.

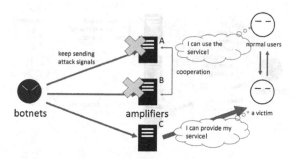

Fig. 3. This figure shows that attackers attack in a constant manner without taking into account alliance among defenders and the defenders are cooperating for mitigating the attacks.

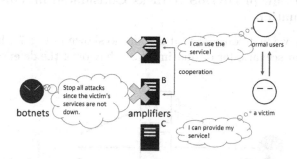

Fig. 4. This figure shows attackers which stop DRDoS attacks when they realize that the attack does not make sense.

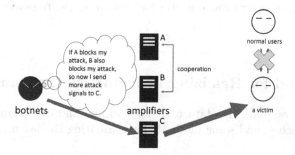

Fig. 5. This figure shows attackers which dynamically change their attacking strategies in consideration of the cooperative behavior of defenders that are on the way of the attacks path.

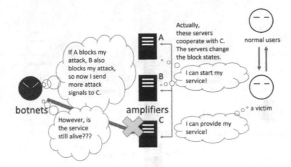

Fig. 6. This figure shows an example of behavior of defenders which attempt to overcome the strategic attacks. Here, the defenders cooperate with "C" in addition to "A" and "B", and then switch to a strategy in which only "C" blocks the attacks when the attackers attempt to send more spoofed request packets to "C".

2.3 An Overview of DRDoS Attacks Considered in This Research for Evaluation

In this research, we first consider that a scenario shown in Fig. 7 which is a minimum experiment scenario for evaluating the behavior of the defense mechanism.

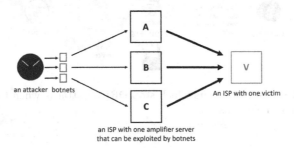

Fig. 7. A minimum experiment scenario for evaluating the response of the defense mechanism

3 A Method for Realizing Learning Mechanisms

In this section, we state the data used for training and evaluating multi-agent learning approaches, and some methods for evaluating the learning mechanism.

3.1 The Need for Dynamic Flow Data Generation

In the evaluation of DDoS attacks mitigation method, the data flowing on actual network environment is often used. For example, Wagner et al. uses data collected at Internet Exchange Point (IXP) [14], Li et al. used data collected at university [7]. However, so far, as Griffioen et al. stated [4], there are few attackers that make sophisticated attacks like changing its behavior considering the defender or network infrastructure. Therefore, the actual data is not appropriate for training or evaluating our learning mechanism that we will develop. Furthermore, for doing machine learning, we need the data for learning and for evaluating the result of learning individually, and we have to consider the data for parameter tuning of learning machine. Therefore, it is difficult for us to gather needed learning data using only real data. In addition, reinforcement learning methods, which we plan to use, require interactions between defenders and the environment in which DRDoS attacks is launched. For the above reasons, we have to dynamically generate the data that represent the attacks that may be done in near future by attackers which dynamically change their behavior based on the environment while DRDoS attacks is ongoing.

3.2 Generating DRDoS Attacks

In our work, for generating the attack data, we consider to generate the network flow that take into account the characteristics of the attackers making DRDoS attacks [4]. As a concrete method for generating the data, we plan to use NetFlow-Generator[1] for generating the network flow, and then reproduce it using nfreplay command[2].

We are also considering the response of the attackers that take the environment related the attacks into consideration. The response is, for example, changing the protocol or amp server (reflector) exploited by the attackers at fixed intervals, increasing the output of some botnets in other ISP when the attackers detect that the attacks done by the botnet in another ISP is blocked by the ISP, and so on.

3.3 Realizing the Filtering Behavior

Since the attackers change their behavior based on the effectiveness of the attacks, we also have to simulate the situation that attacks targeted to a victim are meaningless due to the filtering by the defenders. In addition, the fact that the entire attack environment is taken into consideration when the learning is performed is also reason for realizing the filtering behavior. For performing the filtering response, we consider to employ "PF", which is a system for packet filtering on OpenBSD. Figure 8 shows a situation adding a filtering rule dynamically using PF. Here, we use a simple detection method, which drop packets exceeding a predefined threshold.

---

[1] https://github.com/mshindo/NetFlow-Generator.
[2] https://openports.se/net/nfdump.

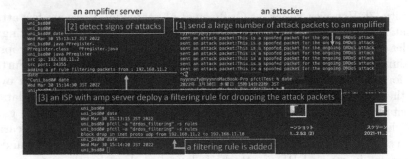

Fig. 8. A situation adding a rule dynamically using PF

3.4   Getting Observation Values

In this research, we consider that the defenders' learning mechanism for mitigating the attacks apply a Markov Decision Process or a Partially Observable Markov Decision Process (POMDP) [1] to their decision making in DRDoS attack environment. Here, since the observation values is required for the model that uses the POMDP, we have to get the observations value in some way. Shinde et al., who employed the interactive partially observable Markov decision process (I-POMDP) [3] for making decisions that take into account the intention of attacker who invade the host in them research, obtained the logs of Linux used as experiment environment for acquiring the observation values [11]. In our work, we also consider using the log data for acquiring the observations. Here, considering that the target of observations value is network traffic and that we will use OpenBSD7.0 in our simulation, we plan to use Packet Filter(PF), which is OpenBSD's system for filtering TCP/IP traffic and doing Network Address Translation[3].

3.5   Realizing a Simulator

In this section, we state how to implement the simulator for generating data representing the attacks that may be done in near future by sophisticated attacker which consider the environment. For realizing the simulator of the DRDoS attacks, we can mainly employ the following three techniques:

(a) representation of the quantitative time variation based on the model
(b) utilization of software simulator
(c) simulation using the network equipments physically

(a) is a method that reproduce the quantitative time variation based on the model using MATLAB and so on. For reproducing the quantitative time variation, some elements such as the strength of the attacks are taken into consideration [6]. (b) is a method that enable us to freely expand the range or condition

---

[3] https://www.openbsd.org/faq/pf/.

Fig. 9. The machines, switch, and LAN cable that will be used in experiment.

in which the packet flow on the network can be observed and reproduced using software simulator. (c) is a method that make it possible to reproduce some detailed mount-specific behavior using actual network equipments physically. In our work, we will conduct our experiments described in (c), since we were able to prepare some physical network server machines.

3.6 The Devices Used for the Simulation

We now plan to use some sever machines, which is utilized in the company running backbone network, and high-speed Layer-2 switch that supports 10GBASE-T. The equipments that will be used in our work are shown in Fig. 9.

Table 1 shows specifications of each equipment. The specification of the used Layer-2 switch is shown in Table 2.

Table 1. The specifications of each used server

Num.	Name	CPU	Memory	NIC
1	Oracle Netra SPARC T4-1	4cores 32threads	32 GB	1Gx8
2	Oracle Netra SPARC T4-1	4cores 32threads	256 GB	1Gx4
3	SPARC S7-2	8cores 64threads	64 GB	10Gx4 + 1Gx4
6	Oracle SPARC T5-2	32cores 256threads	256 GB	1Gx24

Table 2. The specification of the used Layer-2 switch

Num.	Name	NIC
4	QSW-M408-4C	10Gx4 + 1Gx8

4   Experimental Reproduction of Packet Flows of DRDoS Attacks

In our research, we conducted a preliminary experiment for confirming the behavior of the network against DRDoS attacks. In this experiment, we used the server machines numbered as 2 and 6 in Fig. 9, and high speed Layer-2 switch that support 10GBASE-T described above.

4.1   Experiment Environment

We use the same settings which also appeared in [6]. Here we briefly summarize it in this section. The overview of experiment environment is illustrated in Fig. 10. As shown in Fig. 10, there are three attackers and three vulnerable servers as a reflector, and each attacker corresponds to each vulnerable server.

In our work, we used abbreviations T4 and T5 for "Oracle Netra SPARC T4-1 Server(2)" and "Oracle SPARC T5-2 Server(6)" respectively.

Here, as we did in [6], T4 server simulates the victim server agent and the vulnerable server agents, and T5 server simulates the attacker agents. Each agent has a unique IP address and uses it to communicate with the other agents.

Regarding the used switch port, We prepared only one attacker, which has "192.168.11.43" as its IP address, to 10GbE port and the other agents to 1GbE port.

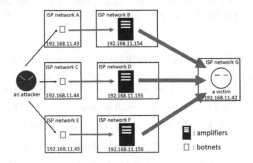

Fig. 10. The overview of this experiment environment for emulating the flow of packets against DRDoS attacks

The procedure to reproduce DRDoS attacks in the experimental environment is the same which we did in [6]. Firstly, each attacker sends a request that set 1048576 bytes (1 MB) cache to the vulnerable Memcached server. The cache size is an initial value of Memcached version 1.6.9 and we assume that the vulnerable Memcached server is in default settings. Then each attacker sends many spoofed GET requests that call the cache data registered by the attacker and continues this attack for approximately 60 s, where each GET request uses only 55 bytes.

As the same way we described in [6], after receiving the GET request spoofed by the attacker, the vulnerable servers respond with 1MB cache registered by the attacker to the victim using UDP protocol per each GET request. In this response, the vulnerable servers divide the sent cache data into 512 bytes and send it to the victim. Note that we omit to implement a detailed spoofing mechanism to make simplicity of implementation and monitoring. We have implemented the amplification behavior on the vulnerable servers as follows: (1) each attacker sends a GET request predefined in the simulation as malicious packets to induce amplifications; (2) a program running as a vulnerable server received the malicious packets to confirm whether the packet is benign one or malicious one; (3) when the packet is malicious one, the program running as the vulnerable server retrieve a cache with "attack" key and send it to the victim.

To capture the packets communicated among attackers, vulnerable servers, and victim, we use an open-source packet capture software tshark[4] on T4 and T5, as we did in [6].

Figure 11 shows a working example which included the attackers, the vulnerable servers, and the victim. The magnified part of the figure shows the output logs running the program of a victim. In the magnified part, "receivedPacketCount" indicates the number of processed packets and "receivedPayloadCount" indicates the received payload's bytes size within approximately one second.

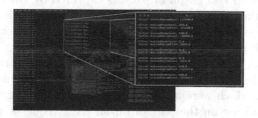

Fig. 11. The running example and the actual log data output of an agent (shown by the magnified part) in our experiment.

For more detailed examples in other parts of the simulation, Fig. 12a (left) shows the GET request packets sent by the attackers to the vulnerable servers in this experiment and Fig. 12b (right) shows a sample response sent by the vulnerable servers to the victim, respectively.

---

[4] https://www.wireshark.org/docs/man-pages/tshark.html.

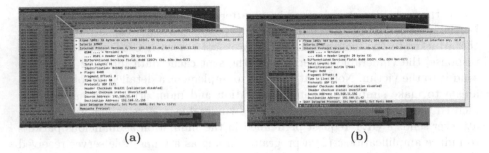

(a)   (b)

Fig. 12. (a) Shows a running example of capturing packets. In the magnified part, a sample of GET request packets sent by the attacker agents in our experiment is shown. Although the mechanism on spoofing the source IP address is not enabled, we can confirm that the amplified packets were sent to the victim by the vulnerable servers. (b) Shows an actual sample of response packets sent by the vulnerable servers to the victim in our experiment (the magnified part).

4.2   Experimental Evaluation

Notice that, as we did in our previous work [6], we prepared a set of pseudo filtering modules that would simulate the ideal behaviors of the filters to be applied.

Figure 13 shows an I/O graph of packets captured by tshark. It can be seen from Fig. 13 that the green line describes the number of packets finally sent by three vulnerable servers to the victim and the purple line describes the amount of packets of GET requests sent to three vulnerable servers to induce packet flows to the victims. In Fig. 13, we can confirm that the vulnerable servers failed to capture the packets sent by the attackers between from 3 to 6 as well as 11 to 15 in the timeline, which were also seen in [6]. While having this limitation on the accurate monitoring on the part of initial GET requests, it is clear that in our experimental environment the amplification of the packets was reproduced in a meaningfully long time (i.e. over 15 s) for further experimentations.

5   Related Work and Discussion

Several approaches have been proposed to detect DRDoS attacks [2,12]. Shurman et al. proposed a deep learning model based on LSTM, able to detect DRDoS attacks [12]. It was trained and evaluated on CICDDoS2019 dataset with various kinds of DRDoS attacks, and the proposed model shows an accuracy higher than 99%. The dataset CICDDoS2019 used in the research is producing realistic DDoS attack dataset including DRDoS attacks [10]. Furthermore, there were some approaches such as a method in which some Internet Exchange Points(IXPs) cooperate [14] and some Internet Service Providers(ISPs) cooperate for mitigating DRDoS attacks [6].

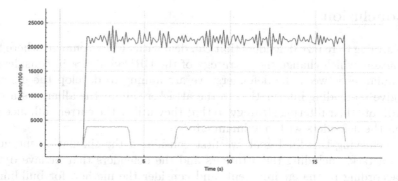

Fig. 13. The green line describes the number of packets finally sent by three vulnerable servers to the victim and the purple line describes the amount of packets of GET requests sent to three vulnerable servers to induce packet flows to the victims. (Color figure online)

When we employ game theoretic aspects in the mitigation approach, it is important to take into account the strategic intention of both the attackers and the defenders. Although some prior works employed game theoretic approaches for the evaluation of DDoS attacks and defense scenarios where the defense mechanisms are deployed [7,13,15], there remained some problems [16]. One of the problems is that most of the previous studies targeted one specific defense mechanism by the defender, in which the defender's decisions lie in how she sets the parameters in the method, and did not consider existence of multiple layers of protection against DDoS attacks commonly deployed in modern enterprise networks [16]. In a real-life DDoS attack and defense incident, the strategic thinking of both the attacker and the defender is affected by many uncertain factors, such as how many legitimate users are using the service, how much traffic is generated from each user, and random packet dropping due to congestion at routers. Standard game theoretic methods such as extensive form games which are commonly used in the previous studies often ignore or simplify possible distributions behind these random events, and thus do not provide a seamless and coherent way of quantifying the effects of these uncertain factors [16]. For dealing with those constraints of game theory domain, Yan et al. developed a game-theoretic evaluation framework [16]. Their framework is able to model different sophistication levels of strategic thinking by the attacker and the defender. Their framework offered great freedom in choosing distributions characterizing legitimate traffic, and provides a seamless method for reasoning among uncertain factors in DDoS attacks and defense [16]. However, the work was using the static game model for their framework, and they stated that extending to dynamic games where decisions of both the attacker and the defender change over time will be their future work. We will work on the construction of the multi-agent learning mechanisms for mitigating the DRDoS attacks that is considering the intention of both the attackers and defenders.

6   Conclusion

We are aiming to realize defenders that can deal with an environment where there are attackers which change their strategy of the DRDoS attack in consideration of the alliance between the defenders, we are aiming to develop the defenders which give misleading information to the attackers about the alliance state and to coordinate their filtering strategy so that they utilize the current alliance state between the defenders with maximum efficiency.

For achieving this final goal, we first considered the simulation method of DRDoS attacks including the attackers and the defenders that behave dynamically according to the environment, and consider the method for building the environment. To realize our idea in the discussion here, we implemented our preliminary prototype simulator and experimentally evaluated it.

References

1. Boutilier, C., Dean, T., Hanks, S.: Decision-theoretic planning: structural assumptions and computational leverage. J. Artif. Int. Res. **11**(1), 1–94 (1999)
2. Gao, Y., Feng, Y., Kawamoto, J., Sakurai, K.: A Machine learning based approach for detecting DRDoS attacks and its performance evaluation. In: 11th Asia Joint Conference on Information Security, AsiaJCIS 2016, Fukuoka, Japan, 4–5 August 2016, pp. 80–86. IEEE Computer Society (2016). https://doi.org/10.1109/AsiaJCIS.2016.24
3. Gmytrasiewicz, P.J., Doshi, P.: A framework for sequential planning in multi-agent settings. J. Artif. Int. Res. **24**(1), 49–79 (2005)
4. Griffioen, H., Oosthoek, K., van der Knaap, P., Doerr, C.: Scan, test, execute: adversarial tactics in amplification ddos attacks. In: Proceedings of the 2021 ACM SIGSAC Conference on Computer and Communications Security, pp. 940–954. CCS 2021, Association for Computing Machinery, New York, NY, USA (2021). https://doi.org/10.1145/3460120.3484747
5. Jin, C., Wang, H., Shin, K.G.: Hop-count filtering: an effective defense against spoofed ddos traffic. In: Proceedings of the 10th ACM Conference on Computer and Communications Security, CCS 2003, pp. 30–41. Association for Computing Machinery, New York, NY, USA (2003). https://doi.org/10.1145/948109.948116
6. Kawazoe, T., Fukuta, N.: A cooperative multi-agent learning approach for avoiding DRDoS Attack. In: Proceedings of 10th IIAI International Congress on Advanced Applied Informatics (IIAI AAI2021/SCAI2021), pp. 518–523 (2021)
7. Li, Y., Li, H., Lv, Z., Yao, X., Li, Q., Wu, J.: Deterrence of intelligent DDoS via multi-hop traffic divergence. In: Proceedings of the 2021 ACM SIGSAC Conference on Computer and Communications Security, CCS 2021, pp. 923–939. Association for Computing Machinery, New York, NY, USA (2021). https://doi.org/10.1145/3460120.3484737
8. Liu, Z., Jin, H., Hu, Y.C., Bailey, M.: MiddlePolice: toward enforcing destination-defined policies in the middle of the Internet. In: Proceedings of the 2016 ACM SIGSAC Conference on Computer and Communications Security, CCS 2016, pp. 1268–1279. Association for Computing Machinery, New York, NY, USA (2016). https://doi.org/10.1145/2976749.2978306

9. Rossow, C.: Amplification hell: revisiting network protocols for DDoS abuse. In: 21st Annual Network and Distributed System Security Symposium, NDSS 2014, San Diego, California, USA, 23–26 February 2014. The Internet Society (2014). https://www.ndss-symposium.org/ndss2014/amplification-hell-revisiting-network-protocols-ddos-abuse

10. Sharafaldin, I., Lashkari, A.H., Hakak, S., Ghorbani, A.A.: Developing realistic distributed denial of service (DDoS) attack dataset and taxonomy. In: Thomas, G.L., John, M. (eds.) 2019 International Carnahan Conference on Security Technology, ICCST 2019, Chennai, India, 1–3 October 2019, pp. 1–8. IEEE (2019). https://doi.org/10.1109/CCST.2019.8888419

11. Shinde, A., Doshi, P., Setayeshfar, O.: Cyber attack intent recognition and active deception using factored interactive POMDPs. In: Proceedings of the 20th International Conference on Autonomous Agents and Multi-agent Systems, AAMAS 2021, pp. 1200–1208. International Foundation for Autonomous Agents and Multiagent Systems, Richland, SC (2021)

12. Shurman, M.M., Khrais, R.M., Yateem, A.A.: DoS and DDoS attack detection using deep learning and IDS. Int. Arab J. Inf. Technol. **17**(4A), 655–661 (2020). https://doi.org/10.34028/iajit/17/4a/10

13. Snyder, M.E., Sundaram, R., Thakur, M.: A game-theoretic framework for bandwidth attacks and statistical defenses. In: 32nd IEEE Conference on Local Computer Networks (LCN 2007), pp. 556–566 (2007). https://doi.org/10.1109/LCN.2007.11

14. Wagner, D., et al.: United we stand: collaborative detection and mitigation of amplification DDoS attacks at scale. In: Proceedings of the 2021 ACM SIGSAC Conference on Computer and Communications Security, CCS 2021, pp. 970–987. Association for Computing Machinery, New York, NY, USA (2021). https://doi.org/10.1145/3460120.3485385

15. Wu, Q., Shiva, S., Roy, S., Ellis, C., Datla, V.: On modeling and simulation of game theory-based defense mechanisms against DoS and DDoS Attacks. In: Proceedings of the 2010 Spring Simulation Multiconference. SpringSim 2010, Society for Computer Simulation International, San Diego, CA, USA (2010). https://doi.org/10.1145/1878537.1878703

16. Yan, G., Lee, R., Kent, A., Wolpert, D.: Towards a Bayesian network game framework for evaluating DDoS attacks and defense. In: Proceedings of the 2012 ACM Conference on Computer and Communications Security, CCS 2012, pp. 553–566. Association for Computing Machinery, New York, NY, USA (2012). https://doi.org/10.1145/2382196.2382255

A Survey of Decision Support
Mechanisms for Negotiation

Reyhan Aydoğan[1,2]([✉])(iD) and Catholijn M. Jonker[1,3](iD)

[1] Interactive Intelligence, Delft University of Technology, Delft, The Netherlands
C.M.Jonker@tudelft.nl
[2] Computer Science, Özyeğin University, Istanbul, Turkey
reyhan.aydogan@ozyegin.edu.tr
[3] LIACS, Leiden University, Leiden, The Netherlands

Abstract. This paper introduces a dependency analysis and a categorization of conceptualized and existing economic decision support mechanisms for negotiation. The focus of our survey is on economic decision support mechanisms, although some behavioural support mechanisms were included, to recognize the important work in that area. We categorize support mechanisms from four different aspects: (i) economic versus behavioral decision support, (ii) analytical versus strategical support, (iii) active versus passive support and (iv) implicit versus explicit support. Our survey suggests that active mechanisms would be more effective than passive ones, and that implicit mechanisms can shield the user from mathematical complexities. Furthermore, we provide a list of existing economic support mechanisms.

Keywords: Negotiation support · Economic decision support · Survey

1 Introduction

Negotiation is part of our daily lives, informally at home or formally in matters of business. We negotiate to reach a consensus if we have a potential conflict of interests [19,43,65]. While some people are very good at negotiation, others have difficulty in reaching optimal outcomes and mostly end up with suboptimal outcomes [56,65]. *When to offer what* in negotiations, is the motivation of this paper and our research objective to support users with the aim to, if possible, obtain settlements that are 1) Pareto-optimal with respect to the preference profile of the negotiators, 2) good for the negotiator that negotiates according to these findings, and 3) that satisfy the additional constraints the user might set. Well-known additional constraints are social wellfare (ensuring that no negotiator is unduly disadvantaged), and timeliness.

Improved negotiation outcomes can be reached by training people before they enter the negotiation, delegating the negotiation to others, or supporting them

---

The authors are alphabetically sorted. They put the same effort.

© The Author(s), under exclusive license to Springer Nature Singapore Pte Ltd. 2023
R. Hadfi et al. (Eds.): IJCAI 2022, SCI 1092, pp. 30–51, 2023.
https://doi.org/10.1007/978-981-99-0561-4_3

during the negotiation. For all of these options, one can either turn to other humans or to artificial intelligence, or to a combination of both. In this paper, the focus is on the use of artificial intelligence, see e.g., [8,33]. We follow Kersten and Lai [35] in using the term e-negotiation system (ENS) to cover the whole set of software systems for negotiation facilitation, support, and automation. We differentiate between analysis and decision support, and between Economic Decision Support (EDS) and Behavioral Decision Support (BDS) when discussing the literature on ENSs, following [22]. We found this differentiation useful as they form two dimensions to study; the need for support and the way mechanisms provide support. For example, the BDS side studies questions such as how to offer support on emotional aspects [15,49], and how to support humans in getting rapport with other human negotiators? On the EDS side belong challenges such as: What is an optimal strategy to reach optimal win-win solutions?

As we report in this paper, support mechanisms can serve as analytical mechanisms that inform both EDS and BDS mechanisms, target behavioral aspects, and/or target economic aspects. For example, the analysis of the economic aspects of a negotiator's preferences can be used to explain the emotional state of a negotiator, whereas a behavioral support mechanism advises the negotiator to make use of economic arguments in their conversation with other negotiators. When supporting or replacing humans by ENSs in experimental settings (cf. [9,21,35]), early successes of improved negotiation outcomes suggest that the EDS systems permit higher joint outcomes and more balanced contracts to be reached, while the BDS systems have a positive impact on negotiator attitudes. However, caution is needed as experimental results reported in Gettinger *et al.* [22] show that these expectations are not always met. In particular, their experiments did not support the hypotheses "More agreements/Better joint agreements/More fair agreements will be reached by negotiators provided with the EDS implemented in the eNSS $\mathcal{N}$egoisst than by negotiators for whom this type of support is not available". Furthermore, contrary to expectations, negotiators supported by a BDS system implemented in the VienNa system were more satisfied with the outcomes but less satisfied with the negotiation process. Given our expertise in system design, these findings lead to the thought that these unexpected (and unintended) results might be caused by the underlying design assumptions or the interaction effect between the mechanisms in the systems. In the remainder of this article, we zoom in on the economic support mechanisms for bidding. Note that we use the words of bidding and offering interchangeably.[1]

Our interest is in the design and engineering of AI technology for ENSs. Thus, our research questions derive from our observation that in the systems' performance, described in the literature, several of the unexpected (and unintended) results might be caused by underlying design assumptions and/or by interaction effects between the support mechanisms. In particular, we found two dimensions that struck us as important. The first is that each existing ENS system captures some negotiation expertise implicitly and others explicitly. In detail, negotiation

---

[1] In the automated negotiation literature the words *bid* and *bidding* are rather common, while in the general literature on negotiation the common word is *offer*.

knowledge or concepts can be exposed to the user implicitly; for example, the concept of utility is not useful for lay people, but can still implicitly be used in the system. However, for trained negotiators, utility is a well-known concept that can be discussed explicitly. We assume that implicit EDS mechanisms in the ENS system can increase the efficiency of the negotiation outcome by shielding the user from mathematical complexities. The second dimension is that some support mechanisms are actively pushed to the user, and some are passively available (can be pulled by the user). We expect that actively pushed support mechanisms are more effective than passive support mechanisms. Based on these considerations, we formulated the following two research questions.

- **RQ-1 Mechanisms:** What economic decision support mechanisms are available for bidding in ENSs?
- **RQ-2 Design:** What choices in the design of economic decision support mechanisms contribute to their success or failure?

Our research method is a combination of a literature study and an empirical study. For RQ-1, we survey and categorize the existing bidding support mechanisms in the literature and study their interdependencies. For RQ-2, we apply three methods: Firstly, we investigate the categorizations of ENSs as found in the literature, as they provide an overall design perspective of ENSs. Secondly, we focus on the economic decision support mechanisms of existing ENSs and finally, we identify the design choices for the existing ENSs and formulate hypotheses on what underlying design considerations potentially influence their effectiveness.

The structure of this paper is as follows. After mentioning the related work in Sect. 2, we review the literature on negotiation (support) systems and extract the bidding support mechanisms and their interdependencies offered by these systems in Sect. 3. The paper ends with conclusions and an outline for future research in Sect. 4.

2   Related Work

There is a wealth of research literature on negotiation, ranging from literature about human negotiations to the use of artificial intelligence to train, represent or support people in their negotiations. The history of research on providing computer support for negotiation is long, actually dating back to the 1960s, see, e.g., [20]. Worth mentioning is the Aspire system [37], which is one of the early negotiation support systems used for training negotiators. There is a steady stream of papers on these topics, with survey papers being published every couple of years, see Jelassi and Foroughi (1989) [27], Foroughi (1995) [20], Kersten and Lai [35], Wang [73], Marsa-Maestre et al. (2014) [45], and Baarslag (2017) et al. [8].

All research on ENS systems relies on insights from the rich literature on negotiation between human negotiators, see, e.g., Harvard's Business school with proponents such Fisher and Ury, e.g., [19], Lewicky [43], and Thompson [65], to name but a few. That literature is vital to understand the participants' behavior and the roles that they might have in a negotiation, be it as a negotiator, as a party represented by a negotiator, participant, as an advisor to a negotiator, or as mediator. Besides the human aspects and attitudes, there is also literature on the mathematical and economic aspects of negotiation, see, e.g., Raiffa and colleagues [56]. Additional insight comes from the literature that uses virtual agents to study human negotiation behavior, see e.g., [42,55]. Furthermore, virtual agents and feedback systems have been developed to train people in predetermined negotiation scenarios, see e.g., [23,28,47].

Reviews of the research on ENS systems show that there are many different aspects of negotiation for which support would be appreciated and that contributes to our overall objective [8,21,22,35,61], with early work dating back to the 1970s, see [51] and the literature survey in Sect. 3. Here, we provide classifications on types of support and an overview of the variety of key functions and tasks of software to benefit negotiations.

The proposal of Gettinger et al. [22] to differentiate between mechanisms for decision support and analytical mechanisms is the basis for the lay-out in Sect. 3, as analytical mechanisms can inform both EDS and BDS mechanisms. The dual use of analytical techniques also explains why the research fields of automated negotiation, see e.g., [6,33,38,59,68], and e-negotiation systems share important research challenges, namely how to deal with uncertainty about the negotiating parties, understanding the domain of negotiation, analyzing and understanding behavioral patterns of the negotiators, see e.g., [8]. The uncertainties negotiators face about the preferences and underlying concerns of the other negotiating parties have economic and emotional aspects. From an economic point of view, gathering more information about the profile of the other negotiators improves the possibilities of offering contracts that the others can accept. From an emotional point of view, reducing this uncertainty in the negotiator's mind potentially reduces stress which in turn enhances the capability of the negotiator to find integrative bargaining solutions. Such insights spur the research on opponent modeling (in particular preference modeling and estimating the opponent's reservation value), see, e.g., [3,6,33,52,68] and strategy recognition [40,74]. Creating a computational profile of the other negotiators is an essential step in other analytical tools, such as the determination of an estimated Pareto Optimal Frontier.

For the research and development of autonomous agents that support humans in negotiation or even autonomously fulfill the role of negotiator, more negotiation aspects need computer-readable formatting. In computer science and artificial intelligence, this is referred to as formal representations, e.g., referring to formal models, formal protocols, and ontologies. In the literature, negotiation process models are distinguished from negotiation protocols, see [39]. Negotiation process models describe the sequence of negotiation activities and phases. Negotiation protocols govern the processing and communication tasks, imposing restrictions and obligations on negotiation activities [18]. Work on formal protocols for negotiation makes it easier for agents to participate in negotiations, either in a supportive role or as automated negotiators, see e.g., [2,46,54,58].

Finally, the work that is most closely related to this paper is that of Chen *et al.* [13], Gettinger *et al.* [22], Schoop *et al.* [61], and Yuasa *et al.* [75,76], as discussed in more detail in the next section.

Formal models and ontologies are used to model the domain of negotiation. They are relevant for supporting the preparations for a negotiation, e.g., by using machine learning for market analysis and discovering patterns in the negotiating behavior of opponents in repeated negotiations. The research questions related to understanding behavioral patterns of negotiators are quite broad in themselves. Two example challenges are the following. Can we detect deception [24,48]? How can agents create rapport with people [12,53,67]? All these examples show that the challenge of developing ENS systems is a complex problem in which support mechanisms might enable other mechanisms and influence both economic decisions as well as behavior decisions. We give a few pointers to the automated negotiation literature: the literature of Automated Negotiating Agents Competition (ANAC) [33], team negotiation by Sanchez [59,60], negotiation for the Diplomacy game [29,30]. The negotiation handbook [46] recommends what negotiation mechanism to use for a given negotiation scenario. An overview of the current challenges in AI for negotiation is presented in [8].

3   Decision Support Mechanisms for Negotiations

We identify the analytical means and decision support (for BDS and EDS) needed for the economic decisions on 1) which concrete offers to make when and 2) whether or not to accept an offer or to end the negotiations without an agreement. We based our findings on literature surveys of the available categorisations of ENS systems. Note that we use the word bidding for what in other papers might be referred to as making offers and counteroffers.

Furthermore, we present an analysis of a literature survey focusing on EDS mechanisms for bidding support and advice. We considered analytical mechanisms that EDS mechanisms might need, and BDS mechanisms that rely on the same analytical mechanisms. Before presenting our survey results, we discuss the categorizations that can be found in the literature.

3.1   Categorizations and Classifications

Reviews of existing ENS systems show that there are many different aspects of negotiation that might be supported. Gettinger *et al.* [22] differentiate between **analysis** and **decision support** and between **economic** decision and **behavioral** decision support. Where analytical mechanisms inform the negotiator, decision support mechanisms provide strategic considerations; advising or critiquing on decisions. Finally, essential functions and tasks of software in e-negotiation should be considered [35,71].

Considering this, we decided to use two dimensions in our categorization. The first dimension entails the type of decisions, for which we follow Gettinger *et al.* [22]: **economic** versus **behavioral** decisions. The second dimension entails the mechanism's intended support of decisions: **analytical** or **strategical**. These dimensions turn out to be quite helpful in our analysis of the available mechanisms in the literature.

Systems playing a more active role on, e.g., making offer suggestions are still rare, as stated by Vetchera *et al.* in [72]. Here, eAgora [13] is mentioned as an exception, demonstrating important points for the design and engineering of ENS systems. For the design, a deliberate choice should be made to integrate the support mechanisms to provide passive or active support. We define a support mechanism to provide *active support* if it pro-actively pushes advice or information to the user in a timely manner. Similarly, we define a support mechanism to provide *passive support* if the support is available upon user request. In our survey, we looked for mechanisms that can provide analytical and/or strategic support and take into account whether that support is provided *actively* or *passively* (upon request). For engineering it shows that the problem formulation, modeling of the preferences, situation, and behavior of the negotiating parties are still difficult for humans and technology.

When studying the literature, we furthermore found, that the difference between providing explicit versus implicit support is essential. How ENS systems structure the negotiation process and organize the interfaces is based on expert negotiation knowledge. In that manner, the system *implicitly* supports the user by highlighting some aspects and takes care of other aspects that the system designers thought do not need the user's attention. For example, the $\mathcal{N}$egoisst interface reduces the negotiator's cognitive load for modeling their preferences and evaluating offers, and Pocket Negotiator (PN) first guides users in becoming aware of their own preferences before asking them to reflect on their opponents' preferences. *Explicit* support is visible in the negotiation and relational concepts that the system uses to present information or discuss negotiation aspects with the user. For instance, $\mathcal{N}$egoisst explicitly displays a utility tracking chart of the offers, EmoNeg provides explicit support on dealing with emotions, and PN explicitly asks for the users' interests in the negotiation. We conclude that design decision about providing implicit versus explicit support, and making it active or passive, are important for the effectiveness of support mechanisms.

We searched for components and mechanisms that correspond to the key functions and tasks software in ENSs as listed in [35], and also functions that come from the literature on automated negotiation [33], what to bid when, when to accept a bid, when to walk away, see [5]. The strategic support mechanisms we included in our survey are those that focus on EDS. That same literature also inspired our search for analytical support mechanisms. Analytical support is about providing information on the ongoing negotiation to the user on both economic and behavioral aspects. Economic analytical mechanisms include, for example, displaying how good the offers are for each negotiating party, preference profiling, which bids were made when (this is called the negotiation dance or history [56]), recognizing the opponent's strategy [40], providing information on where optimal outcomes can be found so that human negotiators can avoid sub-optimal outcomes. Behavior analytical mechanisms are, for example, emotion recognition. Note that all mechanisms for strategic advice rely directly or indirectly on analytical or other strategical mechanisms, while analytical mechanisms only rely on other analytical mechanisms.

In summary, we decided to use the following dimensions for our categorisation of the support mechanisms:

- **D1**: economic versus behavioral decision support
- **D2**: analytical versus strategical support
- **D3**: active versus passive support
- **D4**: implicit versus explicit support

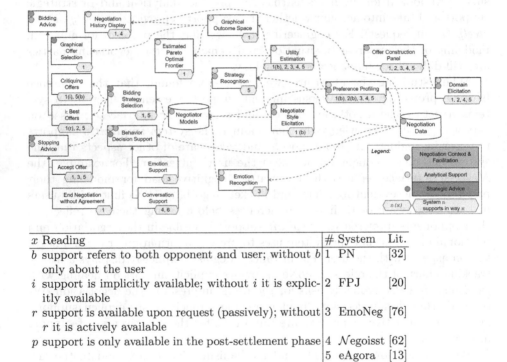

x Reading	#	System	Lit.
b support refers to both opponent and user; without b only about the user	1	PN	[32]
i support is implicitly available; without i it is explicitly available	2	FPJ	[20]
r support is available upon request (passively); without r it is actively available	3	EmoNeg	[76]
p support is only available in the post-settlement phase	4	$\mathcal{N}$egoisst	[62]
	5	eAgora	[13]
	6	VienNa	[16]

Fig. 1. Decision support mechanisms for negotiation

The survey results are presented in Fig. 1, in which the mechanisms are presented in rectangles, the ENSs using them are mentioned in the tags of the rectangles, the dependencies between the mechanisms are indicated by dotted arrows, and the color coding are classifications. In particular, following a dependency arrow from mechanism M to mechanism M' means that the results of M are used in M'. The color coding refers to dimension D2: analytical support (in yellow), strategic advice (in green), and whether the mechanism directly relies on the negotiation context information (in orange). The tags contain two types of information: a number referring to the ENS system and some additional information on the design choices according to dimensions D3 and D4. The tags are further explained in the legend of the figure.

In the remainder of this section, we explain each support mechanism in more detail and discuss whether and how it is used in the ENS systems we found. We explain more about the dependencies and the color labels in the diagram, for which we roughly follow the dependency arrows in the diagram (from right to left).

3.2 Existing Support Mechanisms

In this section, we present the list of support mechanisms from literature that underlie ENS systems in providing Economic Decision Support (EDS). However, as motivated in the Introduction and Sect. 3 some of these mechanisms also enable behavioral Decision Support mechanisms and we categorized these as ENS systems that (also) provide EDS. In comparison with Fig. 1, we roughly work from right to left, going from purely analytical support mechanisms to mechanisms for strategic advice.

To support the user, the ENS needs information about the negotiation context, the domain of negotiation, the user's preferences, if possible, similar information about the other negotiators, and about previous negotiations in similar contexts. The negotiation context is a broad container of topics not covered by the mechanisms discussed below. Information that is part of the negotiation context is, for example, the negotiation's deadline, the cultural background of the negotiators, and the emotional setting of the negotiation. A brief description of each support mechanism shown in Fig. 1 is provided below.

Domain Elicitation. Mechanisms for domain elicitation support the user to establish the issues (also called attributes) of the negotiation, i.e., the aspects to agree upon. Associated with each issue is a range of possible values that have to be identified, next to any dependencies between issues. An interactive user interface is the common form of support for this, occasionally supplemented with information from previous negotiations and from scraping the Internet.

Negotiation History Display and Negotiation Data. Negotiation History Display is a support mechanism that keeps track of and displays each player's offers during the negotiation. Its simplest form is just maintaining a list of past offers made by both participants. Our categorization depends on the more sophisticated variant; *Graphical Outcome Space*, depicting history graphically in the outcome space along with the (estimated) utilities of all negotiators. By analyzing the history of offers, users may understand their opponents' attitudes or strategies better. One of the first to discuss this is Raiffa [56], who called the sequence of exchanged offers; the negotiation dance. We broadened this by including past negotiations to learn more about the opponents' negotiation strategies and typical preference profiles per domain. Several versions are in existence, in PN, also for multi-lateral negotiations, see e.g., GENIUS and the newer GeniusWeb environments [44]. That data needs to be stored in a repository, called **Negotiation Data** in Fig. 1[2]. With the advance of machine learning algorithms, this category gains importance. It is part of the strategic advice and the other support mechanisms to timely share and exploit information extracted from the Negotiation History.

Offer Construction Panel. A basic mechanism, offered by all ENSs with EDS, that facilitates the user in constructing offers.

Preference Profiling. All support on what to offer requires information on the user's interests and preferences. Some systems in addition use similar information about the other negotiators. The essence of preference profiling is to discover what issues are more important than others, and per issue, which values are preferred. In case the system supports interest-based negotiation; also the underlying concerns and interests of the user (and the other negotiator) need to be established. There is a wealth of literature about preference elicitation, see, e.g., [10,14]. We found support for this phase in existing ENS systems, see e.g., [21,32,37]. Additionally, including other negotiators' preferences enables a system to provide more effective advice on what to offer and more insight on current and past offers made by the negotiators. Note that the user might actively do the profiling together with the artificial intelligence, by bringing in their knowledge about the opponent. However, even without human help, artificial intelligence techniques have been developed for modeling the opponent's preferences based on the opponent's offers; see [6] for a survey of such techniques. Presenting the preferences profiles to the user for easy inspection is also useful, see. e.g., [14].

Negotiator Style Elicitation. To most effectively advise the user on strategic decisions, the system would benefit from information on the usual style of the user regarding negotiation. For the system could deploy, e.g., a form of the Thomas-Kilmann conflict-handling mode instrument [64]. For example, it may not help to advise the user to play a hard-ball strategy (not making any concessions) if the user emotionally is not able to do so even if the user would agree that this would be smart in the current situation.

Utility Estimation. Mechanisms for Utility Estimation provide the (estimated) utility of (potential) offers from the different perspectives of the negotiating parties. This functionality is based on the system's mechanism for Preference Profiling and can support the user in making an informed decision about what to offer and what offers to accept or reject. Such a mechanism can be seen as a simple form of the more elaborate critiquing offers mechanism, as discussed below.

Estimated Pareto Optimal Frontier (EPOF). The mechanism for estimating the POF provides insights into which offers are thought to be Pareto optimal. Such a mechanism depends, of course on having preference profiles available of all negotiators. Typically, these negotiators' preference profiles are not available and have to be estimated by preference profiling mechanisms. Presenting the

---

[2] Note that the input comes from many of the mechanisms, but that these input links are not depicted in the figure.

EPOF can be done graphically for bilateral negotiations, but not for multilateral negotiations. In that case, listing the offers on the EPOF together with the estimated utilities for all negotiators might be an option.

Strategy Recognition. Mechanisms for Strategy Recognition aim to help the user recognize their opponent's strategy during negotiation so that user can adjust or refine his actions accordingly. Strategy Recognition for negotiation is still in its infancy. Currently, there have only been a few attempts in this direction; see, e.g., [40]. Maintaining the negotiation history is essential for strategy recognition.

Emotion Recognition. Mechanisms for Emotion Recognition can potentially be deployed to help users recognize their own and the other negotiators' emotional state. There is a wealth of literature on automated emotion recognition, which requires the use of multi-modal sensors to "read" the negotiators. However, using such sensors is ethically questionable. In the systems we found, emotion recognition is basically delegated to the user, whom via the user interface indicates the emotional state of the opponent [11,13]. Such mechanisms can be used to inform behavior decision support mechanisms.

Negotiator Models. We introduced the Negotiator Models repository that maintains all the data on the user and the other negotiators as acquired by the various mechanisms present in a system. From this repository, other mechanisms can extract information to support the user.

Graphical Outcome Space. A graphical representation of the possible outcomes of a bilateral negotiation that plots all possible offers on the space spanned by the utilities for both negotiators. This is only possible if the mechanism has access to the estimated utility functions for both negotiators and to the domain specification. It, therefore, depends directly on the Utility Estimation mechanism and indirectly on the mechanisms Preference Profiling and Domain Elicitation. If the EPOF is to be plotted, it also directly depends on the related mechanism. Having offers depicted in the graph provides easy insight into the use of that offer's efficiency. This would present a potential dependency on Negotiation History Display.

Bidding Strategy Selection. There already exist many competitive bidding and acceptance strategies, see e.g., [1,5,7,33,57]. Given these strategies, one would expect that negotiation support systems would also provide some strategic advice on what bidding strategy to select. So far, we have found no system that does so. Although eAgora [13] and PN let the users set and adjust their negotiation strategy.

Behavior Decision Support. In human negotiations interpersonal relationships are vital. The user may need emotional and conversational support to create rapport with the negotiation partner. There are some studies regarding how facial expressions affect the negotiation process. For instance, experiments have shown that human negotiators concede more when they are negotiating with a virtual agent having an angry facial expression than with an agent with a happy face

[49,70]. Similarly, in the study reported in [25], it is shown that dominant movements and emotional expressions are variables that provide higher scores during human agent negotiations. Yuasa *et al.* present a study in which their ENS system EmoNeg advises the participants on how to adapt their facial expressions to balance the emotions during negotiations. This form of emotional manipulation also enforces in human negotiators how important the negotiation atmosphere is. More information on these aspects can be found at, e.g., the Harvard Business School. The mechanism of EmoNeg is embedded in Fig. 1 under the name **Emotion Support**. Furthermore, mechanisms for **Conversation Support** are available in the $\mathcal{N}$egoisst and the VienNa ENS systems.

Graphical Offer Selection. The Graphical Offer Selection mechanism is related to the Offer Construction Panel mechanism as it also allows the user to construct an offer. However, the mechanism relies entirely on the Graphical Outcome Space mechanism. It allows the user to click on a point in that space, and its underlying offer is immediately constructed as a bid in the Offer Construction Panel. In PN this mechanism is implemented for the EPOF offers only.

Bidding Advice. Mechanisms that provide Bidding Advice, i.e., advice on what to offer or counteroffer, ideally have access to the negotiation context (e.g., to know the negotiation deadline or other constraints), and to the models of all negotiators; not just to the user's model. In particular, the mood and/or emotional states of the negotiators, information on their preference/utility profiles and their negotiation strategies. We found two specific forms of bidding advice in the ENS systems, namely **Critiquing Offers** and k **Best Offers**. **Critiquing Offers** as discussed and used in eAgora [13] is a mechanism that pro-actively critiques offers received from the opponent (e.g., to reject an offer) or that the user plans to make (e.g., that the user is conceding too much) based on a set of critiquing rules. k **Best Offers** is a mechanism that suggests k best alternative offers to make based on the selected strategies and the preferences. Variation is in terms of the parameter k, and whether or not only the user's strategy and preferences are taken into account (user-oriented), or also those of the other negotiators (all-oriented). The mechanism is used in eAgora [13] ($k = 5$, user-oriented), FPJ [21] ($k = 3$, user-oriented), and PN [32] ($k = 1$, all-oriented).

Stopping Advice. We found two explicit mechanisms on stopping the negotiation; **Accept Offer** and **End Negotiation without Agreement**. We found three systems that provide the Accept Offer mechanism, i.e., FPJ [21], eAgora [13], and PN [32]. For an overview of strategies for accepting bids, see [7]. Strategic advice on when to walk away from the negotiation without an agreement is discussed in [34]. Both the advice to accept the offer or to end the negotiation without an agreement can be encountered in PN.

3.3 Available Decision Support Systems for Negotiation

Given the long history of the field of ENSs one might expect fully fledged ENSs readily available to the interested negotiator. However, to date, our search for systems that offer active and concrete support during potentially real negotiations on arbitrary domains and for which peer-reviewed scientific papers are available, returned only the following systems[3]: **FPJ** [20], **EmoNeg** [76], **Aspire** [37], *N*egoisst [62], **VienNa** [16], **eAgora** [13], and **Pocket Negotiator (PN)** [32]. These systems play a major role in our survey and in our resulting diagram, see Fig. 1.

The FPJ System. A negotiation support system with a long history is that of Foroughi, Perkins, and Jelassi ([20, 21]) that offers mechanisms they call Contract Point Evaluator and Decision Tool. Yet, we could not find a current version of the tool. The Decision Tool estimated the point structure of the other negotiating party, which is why the mechanism *Preference Profiling* in Fig. 1 is tagged with a "2" and the parameter "b" indicating a preference structure for both negotiating parties. The Decision tool generated all possible outcomes and ranked them in descending order of the joint utilities (summation), which is why the *Utility Estimation* mechanism has the tag 2(b) as well. In their system, the three bids with the highest joint outcome were displayed to the user, which is a form of the *k Best Offers* ($k = 3$) mechanism. Note that their mechanism was implemented as an active mechanism with the implicit aspect of the suggestion to pick from the three best options. The Contract Point Calculator in [20] allowed people to enter an offer, which is a form of the *Offer Construction Panel*. The Contract Point Calculator calculated the user's score (utility) for that offer, but not that of the opponent. In their experiments, Foroughi *et al.* varied on the competitiveness of the bargaining task, and they showed that their system improved negotiation outcomes and user satisfaction [21].

The EmoNeg System. The EmoNeg system by Yuasa *et al.* [76] provides bidding advice on the height of the offer based on the user's utility function, which means the system has a form of *Utility Estimation* but only from the user's perspective; thus tagged with a "3" without the parameter "b". The paper presents the system for negotiation within the game"Monopoly" and makes no mention of providing support for domain elicitation. However, there is an *Offer Construction Panel*. EmoNeg specialises on *emotion support* on the basis of Newcomb's ABX model [50] to advice humans during negotiations on their next move. The rule-based mechanism for this is based on [66], and by asking the user to perform the task of *Emotion Recognition* from the other negotiator's facial expression.

The *N*egoisst System. *N*egoisst [61, 62] is an ENS system that provides decision support, communication support, and document management as depicted in Fig. 2. In this paper, we only focus on its decision-support elements; however, we tagged *N*egoisst on the Behavior Decision Support mechanism *Conversation Support*. *N*egoisst provides support to the user for preference elicitation and utility estimation, and it displays and stores the negotiation history, as tagged

---

[3] Note that FPJ and EmoNeg are names given to these systems by the authors of the current paper.

accordingly in Fig. 1. We interpret the way that 𝒩egoisst documents and processes the information, the messages exchanged between the negotiators, and the use of the informal "green" and formal "red" workspaces as a form of *Domain Elicitation* mechanism. Messaging is based on Speech Act Theory [63]. The message editor is a form of *Offer Construction Panel* The utility estimation of offers and counteroffers is estimated based on the preference elicitation process giving a utility range for partial offers. The *Negotiation History Display* mechanism shows the estimated utility of previous offers concerning only the user's own preferences. Note that 𝒩egoisst has storage of Negotiation Data and Negotiator Models.

Fig. 2. Bidding interface of 𝒩egoisst [61]

The eAgora System. eAgora [13] is an ENS system for multi-issue negotiations in e-marketplaces. The eAgora agent generates and actively pushes a set of attractive alternative offers to the user (*k Best Offers*, with $k = 5$), actively pushes critique on offers that the user contemplates to submit, and on offers received by the opponent (*Critiquing Offers*) as seen in Fig. 3. eAgora implements *Strategy Recognition* a fuzzy assessment of the concessions of the opponent measured according to the user's utility function. The *Bidding Strategy Selection* allows the user to select "competitive", "collaborative", "compromising", or "accommodating". Furthermore, eAgora implements forms of *Domain Elicitation, Offer Construction Panel, Preference Profiling* (for the user only), *Utility Estimation* (for the user only), *Strategy Recognition*, and *Accept Offer*, see Fig. 1.

The authors motivate actively pushing advice by stating that users do not need advanced technical or decision analytical skills. Presenting a set of top alternatives instead of just one is motivated by two arguments. First, the user

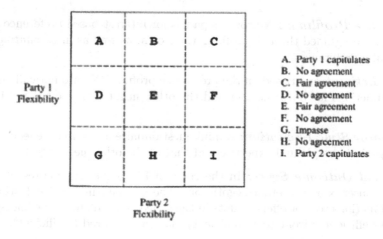

(a) Offer Construction in eAgora   (b) Critiquing by eAgora

Fig. 3. The user interfaces of eAgora [13]

preference model is only an approximation of the user's true preferences, and providing a set of alternatives gives the negotiator a better idea of what good or satisfying offers are like.

The VienNa System. VienNa [16,17] is a mediation support system that collects information on how flexible negotiators are on the negotiation issues and process by using an e-survey. The flexibility score is presented in a grid, see Fig. 4. The system provides interaction advice regarding integrative agreements, fairness, information exchange, and fractionation of issues. Their interaction advice is a facilitation type of support, tagged as the *Conversation Support* mechanism in Fig. 1.

	A	B	C
Party 1 Flexibility	D	E	F
	G	H	I

Party 2 Flexibility

A. Party 1 capitulates
B. No agreement
C. Fair agreement
D. No agreement
E. Fair agreement
F. No agreement
G. Impasse
H. No agreement
I. Party 2 capitulates

Fig. 4. Qualitative analysis of flexibility in VienNa [17]

Pocket Negotiator. The Pocket Negotiator [32] (PN) provides guidance throughout the negotiation process. In this article, we focus on its EDS aspects in the bidding phase. The PN provides the following mechanisms, see Fig. 5:

Fig. 5. Bidding interface of the Pocket Negotiator

Domain Elicitation: PN has an interest-based domain editor for modeling multi-issue bilateral domains.

Offer Construction Panel: A GUI with pull-down menu's per issue to select values.

Preference Profiling: PN provides panels for interest-based preference profiling. Users are guided through profiling their own, as well as in *estimating* their opponent's preferences.

Utility Estimation: Based on the preference profiles PN automatically creates utility functions for both the user and the other negotiator, see the red bars in Fig. 5.

Negotiator Style Elicitation: A mini questionnaire helps users reflect on their own negotiation style and expertise and that of the other negotiator.

Graphical Outcome Space: In the right of Fig. 5 the axes represent utility (y-axis = user, x-axis = other negotiator). The mechanism uses the (estimated) utility functions to plot offers as dots in the space. The colour of the background indicates efficiency: from green (efficient) via orange to red (inefficient).

Negotiation History Display: The offers made by both negotiators are logged and presented as dots in the *Graphical Outcome Space* on the right of Fig. 5. This provides the user with insights in the progress of the negotiation. The user can hover over these offers to see their content in a pop-up window.

EPOF: This mechanism uses the (estimated) utility functions of the negotiators to compute the EPOF, and displays these offers as dots in the *Graphical Outcome Space* on the right of Fig. 5. The EPOF construction depends on the results of the *Estimated Utility* mechanism, which in turn relies on the *Preference Profiling* mechanism and on the *Domain Elicitation* mechanism.

Graphical Offer Selection: The user can click on dots of the EPOF in the *Graphical Outcome Space* as presented on the right of Fig. 5. Selected offers are copied immediately to the *Offer Construction Panel*. Hovering over a dot, causes the contents to be displayed.

Strategy Selection: Users can select the agent and accompanying strategy to support them with bidding and stopping advice. PN offers a range of strategies to pick from, including Tit-for-Tat, Hard Headed, Optimal Conceder, and Deniz, based on the literature [26,31,33,41].

Critiquing Offers: PN provides an implicit form of critiquing offers by depicting the user's utility and that of the opponent through red bars, on the right of Fig. 5. This mechanism depends on the mechanism *Utility Estimation*.

k **Best Offer**: PN provides this mechanism for $k = 1$ passively; in the tag this is indicated by the parameter "r" that stands for "upon request". The mechanism is accessible to the user by clicking on the **Suggest Bid** button (at the bottom of Fig. 5).

Stopping Advice: PN provides active variants of the mechanisms *Accept Offer* and *End Negotiation without Agreement*. The actual advice comes from the supporting agent selected by the user.

Repositories: PN logs the negotiation sessions in a Negotiation Data repository, containing also domain models, preference profiles, negotiator models of both the user and the other negotiator, and a repository of negotiation support agents.

To emphasize, PN users can create offers in three ways: by selecting a value for each issue in the *Offer Construction Panel*, by clicking on offers on the EPOF in the *Graphical Outcome Space*, or by asking for a suggestion ("Suggest bid").

In summary, PN provides passive economic bidding advice with some implicit and nudging aspects. The design choice to make only offers on the EPOF clickable, gently encourages (nudges) users not to make Pareto sub-optimal bids. The *k Best Offers* mechanism is passive as the user has to request it by clicking on the "Suggest Bid" button. The support agent selected by the user actively provides stopping advice to the user.

Other Related Systems. We do not want to end this section without referring to the other excellent systems in the field of negotiation and negotiation support. The Aspire system [37] is one of the early negotiation support systems used for training negotiators. Aspire provides advice to negotiators, but not through generating offers or critiquing offers. The support is text-based, and the system tries to teach negotiators what effect their explanations of their motivation behind their bids might have on their opponents. It is, however, not easy to adapt the system to new negotiation domains and thus not easy to use for real negotiations in changing domains.

The Shaman system [36] is a framework for the construction and operation of heterogeneous systems enabling business interactions such as auctions and negotiations between software and human agents across those systems. It does not provide support mechanisms of its own, but integrates them.

Looking a bit further afield, we recommend the reader also to consider the Social agent for Advice Provision (SAP) [4]. SAP is an agent that models human choice selection using hyperbolic discounting and samples the model to infer the best weights for its social utility function. In contrast to ENS systems, the SAP agent argues with its human opponent to convince the opponent to take actions that are mutually beneficial to the system and the human. SAP explicitly reasons about the trade-offs between the costs to both participants in the selection process based on a social weight. Both the work by [4,69] is relevant for negotiation support systems, as it will optimize the advice that can be given to the human user. One might adapt other ENS systems to advise the human negotiator on potential trade-offs.

4   Conclusions and Future Work

This paper introduces a categorization of potential and existing economic decision support (EDS) mechanisms. The study focused on analytical support and strategic advice. Our survey of the literature revealed that mechanisms can be integrated into the e-Negotiation Support (ENS) systems to actively (push) or passively (available upon request) provide support to the user. Furthermore, the mechanisms can explicitly or implicitly refer to negotiation concepts and knowledge. In literature, we found evidence that the use of implicit knowledge can be beneficial for the user as it can shield the user from mathematical complexities.

Acknowledgment. We like to express our appreciation of Gregory Kersten who made significant contributions for decades to the Negotiation Support System literature. Losing him is a great loss for the negotiation support research community.

This research was (partly) funded by the Hybrid Intelligence Center, a 10-year programme funded the Dutch Ministry of Education, Culture and Science through the Netherlands Organisation for Scientific Research, grant number 024.004.022 and by EU H2020 ICT48 project "Humane AI Net" under contract # 952026. Moreover, this work has been partially supported by the CHIST-ERA grant CHIST-ERA-19-XAI-005, and by (i) the Swiss National Science Foundation (G.A. 20CH21_195530), (ii) the Italian Ministry for Universities and Research, (iii) the Luxembourg National Research Fund (G.A. INTER/CHIST/19/14589586), (iv) the Scientific and Research Council of Turkey (TÜBİTAK, G.A. 120N680).

References

1. Aydoğan, R., et al.: Challenges and main results of the automated negotiating agents competition (ANAC) 2019. In: The Seventh International Conference on Agreement Technologies. Greece (2020)

2. Aydoğan, R., Festen, D., Hindriks, K.V., Jonker, C.M.: alternating offers protocols for multilateral negotiation. In: Fujita, K., et al. (eds.) Modern Approaches to Agent-based Complex Automated Negotiation. SCI, vol. 674, pp. 153–167. Springer, Cham (2017). https://doi.org/10.1007/978-3-319-51563-2_10
3. Aydogan, R., Yolum, P.: Learning opponent's preferences for effective negotiation: an approach based on concept learning. Auton. Agents Multi Agent Syst. 24(1), 104–140 (2012)
4. Azaria, A., Rabinovich, Z., Kraus, S., Goldman, C.V., Gal, Y.: Strategic advice provision in repeated human-agent interactions. Inst. Adv. Comput. Stud. Univ. Maryland 1500(20742), 23 (2012)
5. Baarslag, T., Gerding, E.H., Aydoğan, R., Schraefel, M.C.: Optimal negotiation decision functions in time-sensitive domains. In: 2015 IEEE/WIC/ACM International Conference on Web Intelligence and Intelligent Agent Technology (WI-IAT). vol. 2, pp. 190–197 (December 2015). https://doi.org/10.1109/WI-IAT.2015.161
6. Baarslag, T., Hendrikx, M.J.C., Hindriks, K.V., Jonker, C.M.: Learning about the opponent in automated bilateral negotiation: a comprehensive survey of opponent modeling techniques. Auton. Agent. Multi-Agent Syst. 30(5), 849–898 (2015). https://doi.org/10.1007/s10458-015-9309-1
7. Baarslag, T., Hindriks, K.V.: Accepting optimally in automated negotiation with incomplete information. In: Proceedings of the 2013 International Conference on Autonomous Agents and Multi-Agent Systems, pp. 715–722 (2013)
8. Baarslag, T., Kaisers, M., Gerding, E., Jonker, C., Gratch, J.: When will negotiation agents be able to represent us? the challenges and opportunities for autonomous negotiators. In: Proceedings of the Twenty-sixth International Joint Conference on Artificial Intelligence, pp. 4684–4690 (Aug 2017). 10.24963/ijcai.2017/653
9. Bosse, T., Jonker, C.M.: Human vs. computer behavior in multi-issue negotiation. In: Rational, Robust, and Secure Negotiation Mechanisms in Multi-Agent Systems (RRS'05), pp. 11–24. IEEE (2005)
10. Boutilier, C., Brafman, R.I., Domshlak, C., Hoos, H.H., Poole, D.: CP-nets: A tool for representing and reasoning withconditional ceteris paribus preference statements. J. Artif. Intell. Res. 21, 135–191 (2004)
11. Broekens, J., Harbers, M., Brinkman, W.-P., Jonker, C.M., Van den Bosch, K., Meyer, J.-J.: Virtual reality negotiation training increases negotiation knowledge and skill. In: Nakano, Y., Neff, M., Paiva, A., Walker, M. (eds.) IVA 2012. LNCS (LNAI), vol. 7502, pp. 218–230. Springer, Heidelberg (2012). https://doi.org/10.1007/978-3-642-33197-8_23
12. Cassell, J., Bickmore, T.: Negotiated collusion: modeling social language and its relationship effects in intelligent agents. User Model. User-ADAP. Inter. 13(1–2), 89–132 (2003)
13. Chen, E., Vahidov, R., Kersten, G.E.: Agent-supported negotiations in the e-marketplace. Int. J. Electron. Bus. 3(1), 28–49 (2005)
14. Chen, Y., Qian, J., Wang, J., Xia, L., Zahavi, G.: Opra: an open-source online preference reporting and aggregation system. arXiv preprint arXiv:2005.13714 (2020)
15. Dehghani, M., Carnevale, P.J., Gratch, J.: Interpersonal effects of expressed anger and sorrow in morally charged negotiation. Judg. Decis Mak. 9(2) (2014)
16. Druckman, D., Druckman, J.N., Arai, T.: e-mediation: evaluating the impacts of an electronic mediator on negotiating behavior. Group Decis. Negot. 13(6), 481–511 (2004)
17. Druckman, D., Ramberg, B., Harris, R.: Computer-assisted international negotiation: a tool for research and practice. Group Decis. Negot. 11(3), 231–256 (2002)

18. Faratin, P., Sierra, C., Jennings, N.: Negotiation decision functions for autonomous agents. Robot. Auton. Syst. **24**(3), 159–182 (1998)
19. FISHER, R., William, L.: Getting to Yes. Penguin Group, New York (1981)
20. Foroughi, A., Perkins, W., Jelassi, T.: An empirical study of an interactive, session-oriented computerized negotiation support system (NSS). Group Decis. Negotiat. **4**, 485–512 (1995). https://doi.org/10.1007/BF01409712
21. Foroughi, A., Perkins, W.C., Hershauer, J.C.: A study of asymmetrical decision support in computerized negotiation support systems (NSS). Glob. Bus. Fin. Rev. **20**(1), 25–42 (2015)
22. Gettinger, J., et al.: Impact of and interaction between behavioral and economic decision support in electronic negotiations. In: Hernández, J.E., et al. (eds.) Decision Support Systems - Collaborative Models and Approaches in Real Environments, pp. 151–165. Springer, Berlin Heidelberg (2012)
23. Gratch, J., DeVault, D., Lucas, G.: The benefits of virtual humans for teaching negotiation. In: Traum, D., Swartout, W., Khooshabeh, P., Kopp, S., Scherer, S., Leuski, A. (eds.) IVA 2016. LNCS (LNAI), vol. 10011, pp. 283–294. Springer, Cham (2016). https://doi.org/10.1007/978-3-319-47665-0_25
24. Gratch, J., Nazari, Z., Johnson, E.: The misrepresentation game: how to win at negotiation while seeming like a nice guy. In: Proceedings of the 2016 International Conference on Autonomous Agents & Multiagent Systems, pp. 728–737. IFAAMAS (2016)
25. Gratch, J., DeVault, D., Lucas, G.: The benefits of virtual humans for teaching negotiation. In: Traum, D., Swartout, W., Khooshabeh, P., Kopp, S., Scherer, S., Leuski, A. (eds.) IVA 2016. LNCS (LNAI), vol. 10011, pp. 283–294. Springer, Cham (2016). https://doi.org/10.1007/978-3-319-47665-0_25
26. Hindriks, K., Tykhonov, D.: Opponent modelling in automated multi-issue negotiation using bayesian learning. In: Proceedings of the 7th International Conference on Autonomous Agents and Multi-Agent Systems, pp. 331–338 (2008)
27. Jelassi, M.T., Foroughi, A.: Negotiation support systems: an overview of design issues and existing software. Decis. Support Syst. **5**(2), 167–181 (1989)
28. Johnson, E., Lucas, G., Kim, P., Gratch, J.: Intelligent tutoring system for negotiation skills training. In: Isotani, S., Millán, E., Ogan, A., Hastings, P., McLaren, B., Luckin, R. (eds.) AIED 2019. LNCS (LNAI), vol. 11626, pp. 122–127. Springer, Cham (2019). https://doi.org/10.1007/978-3-030-23207-8_23
29. de Jonge, D., Baarslag, T., Aydoğan, R., Jonker, C., Fujita, K., Ito, T.: The challenge of negotiation in the game of diplomacy. In: Lujak, M. (ed.) Agreement Technologies, pp. 100–114. Springer International Publishing, Cham (2019). https://doi.org/10.1007/978-3-030-17294-7_8
30. de Jonge, D., Sierra, C.: D-Brane: a diplomacy playing agent for automated negotiations research. Appl. Intell. **47**(1), 158–177 (2017). https://doi.org/10.1007/s10489-017-0919-y

31. Jonker, C.M., Aydoğan, R.: Deniz: a robust bidding strategy for negotiation support systems. In: Ito, T., Zhang, M., Aydoğan, R. (eds.) ACAN 2018. SCI, vol. 905, pp. 29–44. Springer, Singapore (2021). https://doi.org/10.1007/978-981-15-5869-6_3

32. Jonker, C.M., et al.: An introduction to the pocket negotiator: a general purpose negotiation support system. In: Criado Pacheco, N., Carrascosa, C., Osman, N., Julián Inglada, V. (eds.) EUMAS/AT -2016. LNCS (LNAI), vol. 10207, pp. 13–27. Springer, Cham (2017). https://doi.org/10.1007/978-3-319-59294-7_2

33. Jonker, C.M., Aydoğan, R., Baarslag, T., Fujita, K., Ito, T., Hindriks, K.V.: Automated negotiating agents competition (anac). In: AAAI, pp. 5070–5072 (2017)

34. Jonker, C.M., Robu, V., Treur, J.: An agent architecture for multi-attribute negotiation using incomplete preference information. Auton. Agent. Multi-Agent Syst. 15(2), 221–252 (2007)

35. Kersten, G., Lai, H.: Negotiation support and e-negotiation systems: an overview. Group Decis. Negot. 16, 553–586 (2007)

36. Kersten, G.E., Kowalczyk, R., Lai, H., Neumann, D., Chhetri, M.B.: Shaman: software and human agents in Multiattribute auctions and negotiations. In: Gimpel, H., Jennings, N.R., Kersten, G.E., Ockenfels, A., Weinhardt, C. (eds.) Negotiation, Auctions, and Market Engineering. LNBIP, vol. 2, pp. 116–149. Springer, Heidelberg (2008). https://doi.org/10.1007/978-3-540-77554-6_9

37. Kersten, G.E., Lo, G.: Aspire: an integrated negotiation support system and software agents for e-business negotiation. Int. J. Internet Enterpr. Manag. 1(3), 293–315 (2003)

38. Keskin, M.O., Çakan, U., Aydoğan, R.: Solver Agent: Towards Emotional and Opponent-Aware Agent for Human-Robot Negotiation. In: Proceedings of the 20th International Conference on Autonomous Agents and MultiAgent Systems, pp. 1557–1559. AAMAS '2021 (2021)

39. Kim, J.B., Segev, A.: A framework for dynamic ebusiness negotiation processes. In: EEE International Conference on E-Commerce, pp. 84–91. IEEE (2003)

40. Koeman, V.J., Hindriks, K.V., Gratch, J., Jonker, C.M.: Recognising and explaining bidding strategies in negotiation support systems. In: Proceedings of the 18th International Conference on Autonomous Agents and Multi-Agent Systems, pp. 2063–2065 (2019)

41. van Krimpen, T., Looije, D., Hajizadeh, S.: Hardheaded. In: Complex Automated Negotiations: Theories, Models, and Software Competitions, pp. 223–227. Springer, Cham (2013). https://doi.org/10.1007/978-3-642-30737-9_17

42. Lee, M., Lucas, G., Mell, J., Johnson, E., Gratch, J.: What's on your virtual mind?: mind perception in human-agent negotiations. In: Proceedings of the 19th ACM International Conference on Intelligent Virtual Agents, pp. 38–45 (2019)

43. Lewicki, R.J., Saunders, D.M., Barry, B., Minton, J.W.: Essentials of Negotiation. McGraw-Hill, Boston, MA (2003)

44. Lin, R., Kraus, S., Baarslag, T., Tykhonov, D., Hindriks, K., Jonker, C.M.: Genius: an integrated environment for supporting the design of generic automated negotiators. Comput. Intell. 30(1), 48–70 (2014)

45. Marsa-Maestre, I., Klein, M., Jonker, C.M., Aydoğan, R.: from problems to protocols: Towards a negotiation handbook. Decision Supp. Syst. 60, 39–54 (2014), automated Negotiation Technologies and their Applications

46. Marsa-Maestre, I., Klein, M., Jonker, C.M., Aydoğan, R.: From problems to protocols: towards a negotiation handbook. Decis. Support Syst. 60, 39–54 (2014)

47. Mell, J., Gratch, J., Baarslag, T., Aydoğan, R., Jonker, C.M.: Results of the first annual human-agent league of the automated negotiating agents competition. In: Proceedings of the 18th International Conference on Intelligent Virtual Agents, pp. 23–28 (2018)
48. Mell, J., Lucas, G.M., Mozgai, S., Gratch, J.: The effects of experience on deception in human-agent negotiation. J. Artif. Intell. Res. **68**, 633–660 (2020)
49. de Melo, C.M., Carnevale, P., Gratch, J.: The effect of expression of anger and happiness in computer agents on negotiations with humans. In: The 10th International Conference on Autonomous Agents and Multi-Agent Systems, pp. 937–944 (2011)
50. Newcomb, T.M.: An approach to the study of communicative acts. Psychol. Rev. **60**(6), 393 (1953)
51. Nyhart, J.D., Gltner, C.: Computer Models as Support for Complex Negotiations. Palala Press (2015)
52. Oshrat, Y., Lin, R., Kraus, S.: Facing the challenge of human-agent negotiations via effective general opponent modeling. In: AAMAS, vol. 1. pp. 377–384. IFAAMAS (2009)
53. Planken, B.: Managing rapport in lingua franca sales negotiations: a comparison of professional and aspiring negotiators. Engl. Specif. Purp. **24**(4), 381–400 (2005)
54. Ponsatí, C., Sákovics, J.: Rubinstein bargaining with two-sided outside options. Econ. Theor. **11**(3), 667–672 (1998)
55. Prajod, P., Al Owayyed, M., Rietveld, T., van der Steeg, J.J., Broekens, J.: The effect of virtual agent warmth on human-agent negotiation. In: Proceedings of the 18th International Conference on Autonomous Agents and MultiAgent Systems, pp. 71–76 (2019)
56. Raiffa, H., Richardson, J., Metcalfe, D.: Negotiation Analysis: The Science and Art of Collaborative Decision Making. Belknap Press (2002)
57. Razeghi, Y., Yavuz, O., Aydoğan, R.: Deep reinforcement learning for acceptance strategy in bilateral negotiations. Turkish J. Electr. Eng. Comput. Sci. **28**, 1824–1840 (2020)
58. Rosenschein, J.S., Zlotkin, G.: Rules of Encounter: Designing Conventions for Automated Negotiation Among Computers. MIT Press, Cambridge (1994)
59. Sanchez-Anguix, V., Aydoğan, R., Julian, V., Jonker, C.M.: Intra-team strategies for teams negotiating against competitor, matchers, and conceders. In: Marsa-Maestre, I., Lopez-Carmona, M.A., Ito, T., Zhang, M., Bai, Q., Fujita, K. (eds.) Novel Insights in Agent-based Complex Automated Negotiation. SCI, vol. 535, pp. 3–22. Springer, Tokyo (2014). https://doi.org/10.1007/978-4-431-54758-7_1
60. Sanchez-Anguix, V., Aydoğan, R., Julian, V., Jonker, C.: Unanimously acceptable agreements for negotiation teams in unpredictable domains. Electron. Commer. Res. Appl. **13**(4), 243–265 (2014)
61. Schoop, M., van Amelsvoort, M., Gettinger, J., Koerner, M., Koeszegi, S.T., van der Wijst, P.: The interplay of communication and decisions in electronic negotiations: communicative decisions or decisive communication? Group Decis. Negot. **23**(2), 167–192 (2014)
62. Schoop, M., Jertila, A., List, T.: Negoisst: a negotiation support system for electronic business-to-business negotiations in e-commerce. Data Knowl. Eng. **47**(3), 371–401 (2003)
63. Searle, J.R., Kiefer, F., Bierwisch, M., et al.: Speech Act Theory and Pragmatics, vol. 10. Springer, Dordrecht (1980). https://doi.org/10.1007/978-94-009-8964-1
64. Thomas, K.W.: Thomas-kilmann conflict mode. TKI Profile and Interpretive Report pp. 1–11 (2008)

65. Thompson, L.: The Mind and Heart of the Negotiator, 3rd edn. Prentice Hall Press, Upper Saddle River (2000)
66. Thompson, L., Medvec, V.H., Seiden, V., Kopelman, S.: Poker face, Smiley Face, and Rant 'n'rave: Myths and Realities About Emotion in Negotiation. Blackwell handbook of social psychology: Group processes, pp. 139–163 (2001)
67. Thompson, L., Nadler, J.: Negotiating via information technology: theory and application. J. Soc. Issues **58**(1), 109–124 (2002)
68. Tunalı, O., Aydoğan, R., Sanchez-Anguix, V.: Rethinking frequency opponent modeling in automated negotiation. In: An, B., Bazzan, A., Leite, J., Villata, S., van der Torre, L. (eds.) PRIMA 2017. LNCS (LNAI), vol. 10621, pp. 263–279. Springer, Cham (2017). https://doi.org/10.1007/978-3-319-69131-2_16
69. Vahidov, R., Kersten, G., Saade, R.: An experimental study of software agent negotiations with humans. Decis. Supp. Syst. **66**, 135–145 (2014).https://doi.org/10.1016/j.dss.2014.06.009, https://www.sciencedirect.com/science/article/abs/pii/S0167923614001833
70. Van Kleef, G.A., De Dreu, C.K., Manstead, A.S.: The interpersonal effects of anger and happiness in negotiations. J. Pers. Soc. Psychol. **86**(1), 57 (2004)
71. Vetschera, R.: Group decision and negotiation support-a methodological survey. Oper. Res.-Spekt. **12**(2), 67–77 (1990)
72. Vetschera, R., Filzmoser, M., Mitterhofer, R.: An analytical approach to offer generation in concession-based negotiation processes. Group Decis. Negot. **23**(1), 71–99 (2014)
73. Wang, Z., Lim, J., Guo, X.: Negotiator satisfaction in NSS-facilitated negotiation. Group Decis. Negot. **19**(3), 279–300 (2010)
74. Williams, C.R., Robu, V., Gerding, E.H., Jennings, N.R.: Using gaussian processes to optimise concession in complex negotiations against unknown opponents. In: Walsh, T. (ed.) IJCAI 2011, Proceedings of the 22nd International Joint Conference on Artificial Intelligence, Barcelona, Catalonia, Spain, July 16–22, 2011. pp. 432–438. IJCAI/AAAI (2011)
75. Yuasa, M., Yasumura, Y., Nitta, K.: Giving advice in negotiation using physiological information. In: Proceedings of the 2000 International Conference on Systems, Man and Cybernetics, vol. 1, pp. 248–253 (October 2000)
76. Yuasa, M., Yasumura, Y., Nitta, K.: A negotiation support tool using emotional factors. In: Proceedings Joint 9th IFSA World Congress and 20th NAFIPS International Conference, pp. 2906–2911 (2001)

Bidding Support by the Pocket Negotiator Improves Negotiation Outcomes

Reyhan Aydoğan[1,2]([✉]) [iD] and Catholijn M. Jonker[1,3] [iD]

[1] Interactive Intelligence, Delft University of Technology, Delft, The Netherlands
C.M.Jonker@tudelft.nl
[2] Computer Science, Özyeğin University, Istanbul, Turkey
reyhan.aydogan@ozyegin.edu.tr
[3] LIACS,, Leiden University, Leiden, The Netherlands

Abstract. This paper presents the negotiation support mechanisms provided by the Pocket Negotiator (PN) and an elaborate empirical evaluation of the economic decision support (EDS) mechanisms during the bidding phase of negotiations as provided by the PN. Some of these support mechanisms are offered actively, some passively. With passive support we mean that the user only gets that support by clicking a button, whereas active support is provided without prompting. Our results show, that PN improves negotiation outcomes, counters cognitive depletion, and encourages exploration of potential outcomes. We found that the active mechanisms were used more effectively than the passive ones and, overall, the various mechanisms were not used optimally, which opens up new avenues for research. As expected, the participants with higher negotiation skills outperformed the other groups, but still they benefited from PN support. Our experimental results show that people with enough technical skills and with some basic negotiation knowledge will benefit most from PN support. Our results also show that the cognitive depletion effect is reduced by Pocket Negotiator support. The questionnaire taken after the experiment shows that overall the participants found Pocket Negotiator easy to interact with, that it made them negotiate more quickly and that it improves their outcome. Based on our findings, we recommend to 1) provide active support mechanisms (push) to nudge users to be more effective, and 2) provide support mechanisms that shield the user from mathematical complexities.

Keywords: Negotiation support · Bidding support · Experimental performance evaluation · User experience analysis

1 Introduction

Negotiation is a way to solve conflicts of interest among stakeholders [5,19,22, 25]. The negotiation outcome highly depends on the negotiation skills of the

---

The authors are alphabetically sorted. They put the same effort.

R. Hadfi et al. (Eds.): IJCAI 2022, SCI 1092, pp. 52–83, 2023.
https://doi.org/10.1007/978-981-99-0561-4_4

involved parties. Reaching optimal outcomes can be difficult, which explains why negotiation sometimes ends with suboptimal outcomes [23,25]. Human negotiators can improve their negotiation outcomes by training before or being supported during the negotiation. Artificial Intelligence applications have been developed for both purposes. For example, Conflict Resolution Agent (CRA) is a virtual agent used to let humans train their negotiation skills [10,11,20,21], and another example can be found in [3].

The research into providing computer support for negotiation dates back to the 1960s, see, e.g., [6]. Regarding computer support for people in their negotiations, the most frequently used term is Negotiation Support Systems (NSS). The definition of NSS, following [8], is "software which implements models and procedures, has communication and coordination facilities, and is designed to support two or more parties and/or a third party in their negotiation activities." Note that the "third" party refers to an independent party, having no stake in the outcome of the negotiation. Gettinger et al. [9] suggest differentiating between behavior decision support and economic decision support, which touches more on the human-to-human relationship and interactions, versus the more mathematical analysis of the negotiation. In this work, we entirely focus on economic decision support mechanisms and their effectiveness in the process and outcomes.

In their 2015 paper [7], Foroughi and co-authors report that the decision support component of an NSS enables higher joint outcomes and more balanced contracts, and the communication and coordination facilities positively influence the negotiator attitudes. Various support mechanisms can be integrated into a negotiation system, each contributing in different ways to their user's negotiations [4,24,26].

The Pocket Negotiator (PN) is a negotiation support system [13]) that aims at helping human negotiators improve their negotiation outcomes by guiding the negotiation process, and with a specialization in bidding support. It provides a list of support mechanisms such as analytical support mechanisms (e.g., utility estimation, graphical outcome space capturing the negotiation history, estimated Pareto Optimal Frontier) and strategic advice mechanisms (e.g., bidding advice). In this paper, we empirically investigate the effect of the PN support on negotiation outcomes and negotiation behavior during bidding. In particular, we aim to get more insight into the interaction between the system and human negotiators. For this purpose, we set up a balanced within-group experiment for supported and unsupported negotiations in which we measured which support options were clicked by the participants; we measured the outcome utility of the negotiations. Finally, we conducted a questionnaire on the user experience.

The structure of this paper is as follows. Section 2 briefly introduces the bidding support of PN. In Sect. 3, we also formulate the hypotheses for the experimental design. The experimental setup is described in Sect. 4. The negotiation results are presented in Sect. 5 and discussed in Sect. 6. The paper ends with conclusions and an outline for future research in Sect. 7.

2   Economic Decision Support for Negotiation by PN

The Pocket Negotiator [15] is developed to provide support in all negotiation phases; from domain and profile elicitation, through bidding, to closing. The research in this paper focuses on the effectiveness of the bidding support by PN. Therefore, we only describe the type of support provided during the bidding, which is summarized in Fig. 1.

Fig. 1. Pocket negotiator bidding Interface.

In PN, the user can create a bid in three ways: by selecting a value for each issue (middle pane), by clicking on the Estimated Pareto Optimal Frontier (in the graph on the right), or by asking for a suggestion ("suggest bid") underneath the middle pane. In all cases, the constructed bid's content is listed in the middle pane. The Estimated Pareto Optimal Frontier (EPOF) is constructed on the basis of the profile elicitation phase covered by another part of PN, see [15]. Whenever the user has created a possible bid, the red bars above the graph on the right side indicate how good that offer is from the perspectives of the user and the opponent. Note that also this is done using the estimated opponent profile.

Furthermore, each offer made by one of the parties is plotted in the graph on the right (i.e., Negotiation History Display). This enables the user to analyse the progress of the negotiation. The user can accept a bid from the opponent or walk away without an agreement by way of the buttons at the bottom of the bidding interface. Either option ends the negotiation and takes the user to the closing phase which is covered by another part of PN not discussed here.

Finally, PN provides *Stopping Advice* to the negotiator. In particular, it advises accepting an offer when its calculations show that the chances of a better offer coming in the future are too low (which is the *Accept Offer* mechanism and suggests to *End the Negotiation without an Agreement* if it feels that the gap between the negotiators is too big, and the opponent appears unwilling to concede enough to get to the Zone of Agreement. The implementations of the *Bidding Advice* and *Stopping Advice* mechanisms depend on the chosen support agent, selected by the user by way of the *Bidding Strategy Selection* mechanism [15]. In the end, it is of course the user who decides whether to accept an offer from the opponent or to walk away without an agreement.

The Pocket Negotiator offers a range of agents that provide bidding suggestions. Well-known bidding strategies from the automated negotiating agents literature have been adapted for this purpose. Behaviour-based strategies, see e.g., [16], adapt their behaviour in response to the bids made by the opponent are used by the Simple Tit for Tat Agent, and Deniz Agent. Variants of concessions are used by e.g., Conceder, Bayesian Agent [12], and Tough Negotiator. Bayesian Agent uses Bayesian models to learn the opponent's preferences. Tough Negotiator only concedes near the deadline and is based on the HardHeaded agent presented in [17]. For our experiments we chose the Deniz agent as it is not easy to characterize by humans and is a negotiator returning Pareto Optimal bids, see [14].

3   Research Hypotheses

Our review of existing systems showed that all systems offer active analytical support for domain elicitation and preference profiling, and then use the information gained by these mechanisms to offer (actively, or passively) some bidding advice, e.g., in critiquing offers, providing the best k offers to make, bidding strategy selection, and on whether or not to accept an offer. Implicit is the choice to only present the best k options from a ranked list of potential offers as is done in FPJ [6] and eAgora [4]. In this manner, this gives an *implicit advice* not to offer lower than these options, or the choice to make only Pareto Optimal offers clickable as is done in PN [15] as this implicitly encourages people to make offers on the EPOF. Note that *explicit* support is visible in the negotiation and relational concepts that the system uses to present information or discuss negotiation aspects with the user.

From a design perspective, it is essential to look for the design deliberations on whether the support mechanisms were integrated into the systems as provide passive or active support. We define a support mechanism to provide *active support* if it pro-actively pushes advice or information to the user in a timely manner. Similarly, we define a support mechanism to provide *passive support* if the support is available upon user request. Overall we see that PN provides some additional forms of implicit support on the efficiency of the bids (EPOF), Graphical Outcome Space, Negotiation History Display), and passive mechanisms to support offer construction (Graphical Offer Selection, and k Best

Offers). We hypothesize that PN support for Bidding Advice would increase the efficiency of negotiation outcomes and that PN is beneficial for the negotiation experience of its users.

- **H1:** Better agreements will be reached by negotiators provided with PN support than when they do not have PN support.

Chen *et al.* [4] deliberately provide active support mechanisms and argue this to be more natural for potential users as it does not require advanced technical or decision analytical skills, suggesting that passive support mechanisms may require some technical and decision analytical skills. Thus, it might be the case that the mechanisms of PN for *Bidding Advice* will be used differently by users with different backgrounds, and that this effect might be more prominent for the passive mechanisms. In general, we would expect that effective usage of the Bidding advice mechanisms of PN requires a threshold level of technical skills as well as some negotiation knowledge and expertise. Our working hypotheses are as follows.

- **H2:** The utility gain for participants provided with Bidding Advice support mechanisms depends on their background.
- **H3:** The usage of passive Bidding Advice mechanisms by the participants is sub-optimal.
- **H4:** Bidding advice mechanisms that implicitly make use of negotiation knowledge nudge the user towards more effective negotiations.

We test these hypotheses only for PN and in our analysis of the data, we consider differences in the background of the participants. To research our hypotheses, we chose the experimental research approach elaborated in the next section.

4   User Experiments

In order to evaluate the bidding support of the Pocket Negotiator, we created a particular version of the system in which all support options are inaccessible for the user. This allows us to set up a balanced experiment in which participants get the opportunity to experience the system both with and without support. This section explains our experimental setup, the changes to PN to carry out the experiment, and the evaluation metrics used.

4.1   Experimental Setup

To properly test the system, we looked for a domain of negotiation that people are familiar with, so that they can easily engage in the negotiation. We hypothesize that negotiation support becomes more important for people with the increase of the complexity of the domain. So, when facing the choice of a negotiation domain, we were looking for a domain with several issues, but that is still relatively simple. The job negotiation domain we settled on satisfies these criteria. In the job negotiation, we ask people to identify themselves with the role of the applicant that has to negotiate on the following issues: salary (range 2000 till 5000 euro), full-time equivalent (ranging from 0.6 to 1.0), work from home (0, 1 or 2 days), lease car (yes/no), permanent contract (yes/no) and career development opportunities (low, medium, high). We provided the participants with a complete specification of their own preferences, and with what they were told is an **estimate** of the other party's preferences, see Appendix A for the whole story.

In real life, proper preparation for a negotiation entails doing your best to acquire that estimate. The agents underlying the framework have their own approaches to model the opponent's preferences during the negotiation (and more work is currently being done in the research community to learn these preferences also from previous negotiations). To test our hypothesis, we did not want to potentially confuse our results with participants having incorrect or incomplete information on their opponent.

To research our hypotheses, we chose an experimental research approach with three groups with different backgrounds: Computer Science (CS) students, Industrial Engineering (IE) students, and Business Administration (BA) students. CS students have high analytical and technical skills and were given only one lecture on negotiation and ENS systems. IE students are similar to CS students, but we did not provide them with the lecture we gave to the CS students. BA students have less training in technical skills but high negotiation knowledge/skills, as they already had attended several lectures on negotiation, and we gave them the same lecture on negotiation and ENS systems as we gave to the CS students.

The Computer Science students (Group 1) were from Özyeğin University (Turkey), that we motivated to participate by a promise of a bonus point to their overall grade for a course in Collective Decision Making in Multi-Agent Systems. Group 2 consists of Industrial Engineering students from Özyeğin University (Turkey). They were just asked to volunteer, and there was no other connection to the researchers. Group 3 consists of business administration students from Erasmus University (The Netherlands). The Erasmus students were asked to participate in the experiment as a way to get some insight into negotiation tools. There was no relation to their participation and their grade, nor did the researchers have any other connection to the students than just for presenting the negotiation tools and conducting the experiment.

4.2 The Adaptation of PN for the Support and No-Support Conditions

For our experiments, we had to adapt PN to accommodate the No-support condition. In the unsupported version of PN, the users only have the middle section of Fig. 1 available, where they can enter their offers. The red bars, the graph, and the button to ask for a suggestion are not available.

4.3 Evaluation Metrics

The evaluation metric for the performance of the participants was individual utility scored at the end of a negotiation. The utility of outcomes was automatically computed by the Pocket Negotiator system on the basis of the profile information given in Appendix A. Furthermore, we evaluate the effectiveness of the support in terms of the number of bids made on the Pareto Optimal Frontier [23]. Finally, we measure to what extent the participants use the biding advice mechanisms provided by PN by counting their clicks on the k *Best Offers* ($k = 1$) mechanism indicated by the button "Suggest Bid" and the Graphical Bid Selection mechanism. We run statistical tests to study their usage and effect.

In addition to the objective evaluation metrics, we consider subjective metrics as well. After their negotiation experience, we asked the participants about the usability of the PN, how PN influenced their negotiation process in terms of efficiency of the outcome, speed of the process, whether it distracted them, the overview they had of the process, their satisfaction level at the end of each negotiation, and what they think about their opponent in the negotiation. The evaluation of the subjective evaluation metrics was done using a questionnaire on which we ran an ANOVA analysis; see Appendix B for details.

5 Results

In this section, we present the results of the user experiments, first focusing on negotiation outcomes (Sect. 5.1). In the results, we provide the negotiation performance of the participants per group and the overall performance in each condition: *Support* and *No-Support*. Then, we study the usage of strategic bidding support mechanisms in Pocket Negotiator namely Graphical Offer Selection and Bidding Advice (Sect. 5.2). Finally, the results of the participant questionnaire are presented (Sect. 5.3).

5.1 Negotiation Outcome Results

We first present the outcome analysis to study the effect of bidding support mechanisms in PN per group, and then the overall analysis.

Results of Group 1 - Computer Science Students: The first group consisted of 24 Computer Science students (master and bachelor) at Özyeğin University participated in our experiments. The students received one lecture on the main challenges in negotiation and in building automated negotiating agents before participating in the experiment. Figure 2 shows the utilities gained by the participants against the same opponent at the end of their negotiations in both settings. The participants numbered 1 through 12 started with the *Support* condition, and the rest of the participants started with the *No-Support* condition. It can be seen that most participants received more utility when they negotiated with support (blue lines in the graph) than when they negotiated without support (orange lines). Three participants ended with the same bid (thus same utility). Two participants (nr 3, and nr 21) did better without support, while the rest did better with support.)

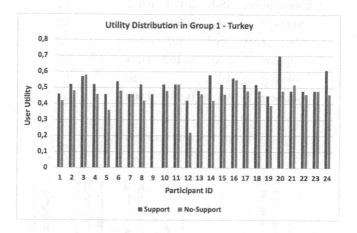

Fig. 2. Utility distribution of Group 1 (CS)

Table 1 shows the average of the utilities received by the users in the *Support* and *No-Support* conditions. According to the Kolmogorov-Smirnov test, the data is not normally distributed; therefore, we applied a non-parametric test, namely Wilcoxon Signed-Rank test. With 0.95 confidence level, the utility received by the participants in the *Support* and *No-Support* versions are statistically significantly different ($z = -3.7191$ and $p = 0.002 < 0.05$), and on average, the users gained higher utilities when supported by PN. That is, the first hypothesis H1 holds for Group 1. In order to see whether the learning effect between sessions plays an important role on the negotiation results, we tested the performance of the participants by grouping them according to their start condition (S-NS denoting *Support* first and then *No-Support*, and NS-S denoting *No-Support* first and then *Support*). The non-parametric statistical test namely Mann-Whitney U test shows no statistically significant difference with a 0.95 confidence level ($p > 0.05$).

Results of Group 2 - Industrial Engineering Students: The second group consisted of 22 Industrial Engineering students at Özyeğin University who did not attend any negotiation lecture prior to the experiment. Figure 3 shows the utilities gained by the participants in both conditions. The participants numbered 1 through 11 started with the PN *Support* condition (S-NS), and the rest of the participants started with the *No-Support* condition (NS-S). Two participants failed to find an agreement in both sessions, and two participants ended with the same offer (thus same utility). Ten participants received higher utility with support, whereas eight participants got higher utility without support.

60 R. Aydoğan and C. M. Jonker

Table 1. Utility: means and standard deviations for Group 1 (CS). Higher mean values are presented in bold face.

Condition	Order	Mean	Std. deviation	N
No support	NS-S	0.470	0.041	12
Support	NS-S	**0.532**	0.071	12
No support	S-NS	0.407	0.156	12
Support	S-NS	**0.497**	0.044	12
No support	All	0.438	0.116	24
Support	All	**0.515**	0.060	24

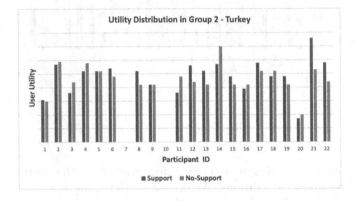

Fig. 3. Utility distribution of Group 2 (IE)

Table 2 shows the average of the utilities received by the participants in the *Support-* and *No-Support* conditions. Since the data for *No-Support* condition was not normally distributed, we applied a non-parametric test, namely Wilcoxon Signed-Rank test. According to this result, there is no statistical significant difference ($z = -1.0017$ and p-value $= 0.317 > 0.05$). The first hypothesis does not hold for Group 2. Similarly, there is no significant difference between the NS-S and S-NS conditions.

Table 2. Utility: means and standard deviations for Group 2 (IE)

Condition	Order	Mean	Std. deviation	N
No support	NS-S	0.457	0.120	11
Support	NS-S	**0.506**	0.145	11
No support	S-NS	**0.385**	0.206	11
Support	S-NS	0.375	0.204	11
No support	All	0.421	0.169	22
Support	All	**0.440**	0.185	22

Results of Group 3 - Business Administration Students: This group consisted of 34 Business students at Erasmus University in The Netherlands. These students have a strong background in negotiation, having followed a course of several lectures on negotiation before participating in the experiment. The experiment took place during one of the last lectures of that course. Figure 3 shows the utilities gained by the participants in both conditions. The participants numbered 1 through 19 started with the *Support* condition (S-NS), and the rest with the *No-Support* condition (NS-S). The results show that 16 out of the 34 participants received a higher utility when they negotiated with support from the PN (blue lines) than when they negotiated without support (orange lines), 8 did better without support, and eight performed equally well with and without support.

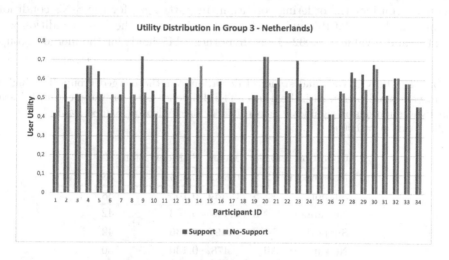

Fig. 4. Utility distribution of Group 3 (BA)

Table 3 shows the average of the utilities received by the participants in the *Support*- and the *No-Support* conditions. According to the Kolmogorov-Smirnov test, the data is normally distributed; therefore, we applied the paired-samples t-test. With 0.95 confidence level, the utility received by the participants in the *Support* and *No-Support* versions are not statistically significantly different (t= −1.741, p = 0.09 > 0.05). Hypothesis H1 does not hold for this group.

Overall Results: In this section, we compose the result for the different groups to allow comparisons between the groups, and we merge the groups to analyze the effects of PN support for the merged group. By merging the groups, we obtain a merged group of size 80, with mean utility results as presented in Table 4. For the merged group, the average utility gained in the PN support condition is statistically significantly different than the one in the no-support condition (p <

Table 3. Utility: means and standard deviations of Group 3 (BA)

Condition	Order	Mean	Std. deviation	N
No Support	NS-S	0.564	0.075	15
Support	NS-S	**0.582**	0.086	15
No Support	S-NS	0.528	0.066	19
Support	S-NS	**0.552**	0.076	19
No Support	All	0.544	0.072	34
Support	All	**0.565**	0.081	34

0.05) irrespective of their starting condition (i.e., S-NS or NS-S). The same holds when we consider the ordering condition. In particular, for the S-NS condition we obtained z = −2.0195 and p-value = 0.043 and for the NS-S condition z = −3.1159 and p-value = 0.002. Thus, hypothesis **H1** holds for the merged group.

Table 4. Utility: means and standard deviations for the merged group. The higher mean values are presented in bold face. The difference between the mean utilities in the two conditions is significant according to the Wilcoxon Signed-Rank Test (z = −3.6011 and p = 0.0003 < 0.05).

Condition	Order	Mean	Std. deviation	N
No support	NS-S	0.503	0.095	38
Support	NS-S	**0.544**	0.105	38
No support	S-NS	0.456	0.153	42
Support	S-NS	**0.490**	0.136	42
No support	All	0.478	0.130	80
Support	All	**0.516**	0.125	80

Even though we can conclude that for the merged group PN support improves the utility gained by the participants, when considering the data in Figs. 2, 3, and 4, clearly this was not true for all participants. In Group 3, about half of them (16 out of 34) did better with support from PN than without, 10 out of 34 did just as well with as without support, and 8 participants did better without support, see Table 5 for more details.

Table 5. The times that negotiation outcomes improved with support (S)

	S>NS	S<NS	S = NS	No agreement	Totals
Group 1 (CS)	19	2	3	0	24
Group 2 (IE)	10	8	2	2	22
Group 3 (BA)	16	8	10	0	34
Totals	44	18	15	2	80

Finally, we checked the utility difference Δ gained by each participant when they negotiated with and without PN support. We define $\Delta = U_S - U_{NS}$, where U_S and U_{NS} denote the utility obtained in the S and NS condition respectively for the same individual. Figure 5 presents the Box and Whisker plot for this data. There is a statistically significant difference between the utility difference in Group 1 and Group 3, as seen in Table 6. These results support for PN hypothesis **H2:** "The utility gain for participants provided with Bidding Advice support mechanisms depends on their background.".

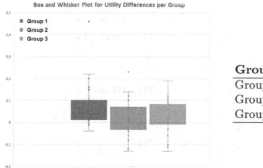

Box and Whisker Plot for Utility Differences per Group

Group	Q1 Δ	Q2 Δ	Q3 Δ
Group 1	0.018	0.040	0.100
Group 2	-0.030	0.000	0.060
Group 3	0.000	0.000	0.075

Fig. 5. Utility gain: group quartiles, where $\Delta = U_S - U_{NS}$

Table 6. Utility gain for Bidding Advice support by PN, according to the Mann-Whitney U test. Note that, regarding Group 1 versus Group 2, the one-tailed test did indicate a significant difference (z = score = 1.77019 and p = .03836 <.05).

Group A	Mean Δ_A	Group B	Mean Δ_B	z-score	p-value
Group 1 (CS)	0.08	Group 2 (IE)	0.02	−1.786	0.074 > 0.05
Group 1 (CS)	0.08	Group 3 (BA)	0.02	−1.973	0.049 < 0.05
Group 2 (IE)	0.02	Group 3 (BA)	0.02	−0.313	0.754 > 0.05

5.2   Usage of Bidding Support Mechanisms

The Pocket Negotiator was developed with the aim to help humans optimize their negotiation results and at least to avoid leaving money on the table by making Pareto sub-optimal bids. Our experiments show that indeed the number of sub-optimal offers is reduced when people use PN. We measured this by logging how many offers made by the participant were Pareto Optimal. The averages per group and condition are presented in Table 7, along with the results of the Wilcoxon signed-Rank test for dependent variables[1]. The difference between the *Support-* and the *No-Support* condition are significant at the level of $p < 0.05$ interval at the group level, even when checking for the starting conditions. The exceptions are Group 2 and Group 3; for the sub-group that started with support (NS-S condition) the difference was not statistically significant.

Table 7. Pareto efficiency: average number of participant offers on the POF per group, per starting-condition, and per condition, and their statistical significance according to the Wilcoxon test.

Wilcoxon Test	S-Pareto	NS-Pareto	z value	p-value	Sig. at p .05
Group 1	7.0	2.3	−3.9199	.00008	✓
Group 2	3.6	1.8	−2.5854	.0096	✓
Group 3	6.4	2.9	−3.7231	.0002	✓
Group 1					
NS-S	6.4	2	−2.6656		✓
S-NS	7.7	2.6	−2.9341	.00338	✓
Group 2					
NS-S	4.6	2.3	−1.6803		×
S-NS	2.6	1.4	−2.1704		✓
Group 3					
NS-S	6.3	2.8	−1.956	.05	×
S-NS	6.6	3	−3.1953	.00138	✓
All Groups					
NS-S	5.84	2.39	−3.7573	.00016	✓
S-NS	5.86	2.45	−4.8467	.00001	✓

The increase in Pareto efficiency cannot be attributed to an ordering effect. Running a non-parametric statistical test namely the Mann-Whitney U test for independent means on the average number of Pareto Optimal offers in the *Support* condition shows that the difference over the (NS-S) versus the (S-NS) condition is not statistically significant at $p < .05$, see Table 8.

---

[1] Note that some p-values are not specified due to the fact that the test is not able to give the actual p values because of a low number of samples. For those results, the W value is lower than the W-critical value.

Table 8. Comparing pareto efficiency over the (NS-S) and (S-NS) conditions. Presented are the average number of Pareto optimal offers in the merged group. The differences are not statistically significant according to the Mann-Whitney U test.

All groups	NS-S	S-NS	z-score	p-value	Significance at p. 05
S-Pareto	5.84	5.86	−0.10598	.912	×
NS-Pareto	2.39	2.45	1.27176	.204	×

Furthermore, we ran Spearman Rho's tests on the correlation between the number of Pareto Optimal bids and the number of times that the participant used the Graphical OfferSelection. According to the results ($r_s = 0.612$ and p-value $= 0$), the correlation with the number of Graphical OfferSelection and the number of Pareto Optimal bids made by the participants is significant. Note that the number of times that participants used the Graphical OfferSelection mechanism is on average *higher* than the number of Pareto Optimal offers made by the participant, see Table 7. This suggests that the participants use the Graphical OfferSelection mechanism and the "Suggest Bid" (k Best Offer) mechanism as a way to explore their options.

Table 9. Marginal means per group and for the merged group. Pareto optimality versus explicit use of clicks to obtain that optimality.

Group	Bids	Pareto optimal	Graphical offer selection	Bid suggestion
Group 1	10	7	8.5	1
Group 2	9.6	3.6	4.9	1.1
Group 3	11.1	6.4	6.7	3.8
All	10.3	5.9	6.7	2.2

In light of hypotheses **H3** and **H4**, we analyzed the difference in how people from the different groups used the passive and implicit Bidding Support mechanisms, see Table 9. For the merged group Fig. 6a and Fig. 6b show how many participants made how much use of the implicit Graphical Offer Selection mechanism by clicking on the EPOF and how often they asked for bidding suggestions (k Best Offers) respectively. These figures show that the clickable mechanisms were not used optimally (some participants never used them at all, and a good portion of the participants only used one of both mechanisms). On the other hand, we also see that some people used these mechanisms more than 10 times, which is more than the number of rounds would account for[2]. The logical follow-up question is, did the people that use these clickable mechanisms get better negotiation results?

---

[2] The default setting for the negotiation was 10 rounds.

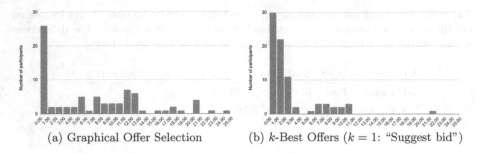

(a) Graphical Offer Selection   (b) k-Best Offers ($k = 1$: "Suggest bid")

Fig. 6. The number of participants that clicked/asked for a specific number of times on the specific support mechanism

In other words, can we find out which Bidding Advice mechanism has the most considerable effect on the increase in utility? Table 10 shows the average utility of those participants that made no use of the clickable bidding support mechanisms at all (None), those that only clicked on the Graphical Offer Selection - which corresponds to the offers on the Estimated Pareto Optimal Frontier - (Graphical only), those that only clicked on "Suggest bid" (Suggestions only), those that clicked on both (Both), and the accumulated set of participants that clicked on any of the clickable Bidding Advice mechanisms (Any). The checked for statistically significant differences between the utilities of these sets, see Table 11. Note that the data is normally distributed according to the Kolmogorov-Smirnov test; thus, we applied a t-test for two independent means. From these two tables, one can see that being able to click on the Estimated Pareto Optimal Frontier by way of the Graphical Offer Selection mechanism had the biggest impact on the utility. However, there was no significant difference between that mechanism and the "Suggest bid" (k Best Offers).

Table 10. Statistical information on the average utility and the usage of bidding support mechanisms. "Both" refers to using both the Graphical Offer Selection mechanism and the "Suggest bid" button (k Best Offers mechanism), while "Any" refers to using either of these.

	None	Graphical only	Suggestion only	Both	Any
# of Participants	9	21	18	32	71
Average Utility:	0.42	**0.54**	0.51	0.53	0.53
Standard Dev.:	0.21	0.07	0.10	0.13	0.11

Table 11. Statistical analysis of the effect of using (combinations of) Bidding Advice mechanisms. Results that are significant at $p < 0.05$ are bold.

Support mechanisms compared	t-value	p-value
None versus anything	−2.62009	**.010561**
None versus graphical offer selection & Suggest bid	−2.0418	**.047976**
Graphical offer selection only versus suggest bid only	0.85413	.398528
None versus graphical offer selection only	−2.35534	**.025744**
None versus suggest bid only	−1.65183	.111076

5.3 Results of the Participant Questionnaire

After completing the negotiations, all participants were asked to fill in an online questionnaire. The questions are renumbered and available in Appendix B, along with the full ANOVA analysis of its results. In this section, we discuss the results of three clusters of questions. The first cluster concerns the impact of the PN bidding support mechanisms on the behavior of the participants. The second cluster focuses on the experience of negotiating with PN support. The third cluster researches the usability of the bidding support of PN. The results of the remaining questions are discussed in [14], which shows that the participants found the Deniz agent to be competitive and that it did not seem human-like to them.

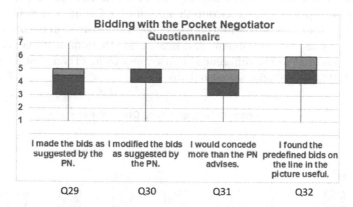

Fig. 7. Participant's bidding behaviour with the PN where value of 1 indicates total disagreement, value of 4 is neutral, and value of 7 is total agreement.

Figure 7 presents the results of questions Q29, Q30, Q31, and Q32. The graphs show that the participants sometimes made bids as suggested by PN (Q29) and sometimes modified the suggested bids (Q30). So, apparently, some of the participants who asked for a recommendation, felt the need to modify these bids. This provides a possible explanation of the results, namely, that the effectiveness of the bidding advice by PN was reduced due to the participants' modifications of those suggestions. This hypothesis is supported by the responses to Q31, namely that the participants indicate that sometimes they concede more than the PN advice. Of course, their thinking about these modifications in itself might already help the participants to get better negotiation results.

The results of Q32 are also of interest to this discussion. Namely, Fig. 7 shows that the participants found the predefined bids of the Graphical Offer Selection mechanism on the EPOF, useful. This result corresponds well with the positive Pearson Correlation between the number of clicks on the EPOF through the Graphical Offer Selection mechanism with the utility that the participants scored in the negotiation. Combining all these results, we hypothesize that the participants felt that the recommendations made by the PN were sometimes too hardheaded (causing them to modify the bids), and that the Graphical Offer Selection mechanism makes it easier for them to make a concession that fits with their own bidding strategy. Note that even if the participants do not use either the Graphical Offer Selection mechanism or the k Best Offers mechanism, they still see where their bid is in bidding space by means of the Graphical Outcome Space mechanism, and how good that bid would be for them and for their opponent in the Fig. 1 because of the Critiquing Offers mechanism implemented in the form of the red bars. The gain that PN support provides to these participants is that it helps them to Pareto optimize their offers, and thus protects them from"leaving money on the table".

The responses on question Q14 ("The Pocket Negotiator improves my negotiation outcomes") in Fig. 9 are consistent with the utilities scored by the different groups. The groups return a statistically significant difference in responses. The average for Group 1 is 4.5, for Group 2: 4.9, and for Group 3: 3.8. Group 3 was the group that had taken part in a course of several lectures on negotiation prior to participating in the experiment, and indeed, for them on average, the benefit of the PN, measured as the difference in outcome was less than that for the other groups (NS: 0.544, S: 0.565, see also Table 3).

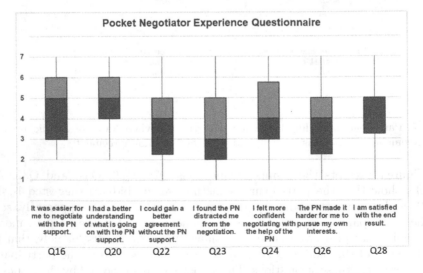

Fig. 8. Participants' negotiation experience with the PN

We also asked the participants about the quality of their experience with PN, see Fig. 8. We conclude that the participants found that PN made it easier for them to negotiate, and that they gained a better understanding of what is going on in the negotiation. Note that the following questions were phrased negatively. Therefore, average low-scored responses indicate that in fact they found the PN useful:

Q21: Neutral - average 4.1, median 4
Q22: Neutral - average 3.9, median 4
Q23: Positive - average 3.5, median 3

The answers to the positively phrased Q24 "I felt more confident negotiating with the help of the PN" (average 4.3, median 4), shows that PN did not raise their confidence in the negotiation sessions. Overall, the participants were somewhat satisfied with the final result (Q28) (average of 4.6 and a median of 5). Note that this last question might also reflect on their satisfaction with their own results and not necessarily on the support by PN.

The variable *group* had a statistically significant effect on the responses to Q22, which on average had a neutral answer. To understand this, we looked at the average responses per group: Group 1 (average 3.1), Group 2 (average 4.2), Group 3 (average 4.3). We see again that Group 1 appreciated PN better than Group 3. Furthermore, the larger group size of Group 3 influences the median and average of the merged group. This effect also applies to Q23, where the averages per group are: Group 1: 2.7, Group 2: 3.8, Group 3: 3.8.

When asked about the statement "The PN improves my negotiation outcomes" (Q14), the participants' responses are on average somewhat positive (average 4.3, median 4.9), see Fig. 9, and in this again, the group differences are statistically significant: the averages for these groups are: Group 1: 4.5, Group 2: 4.9, Group 3: 3.8.

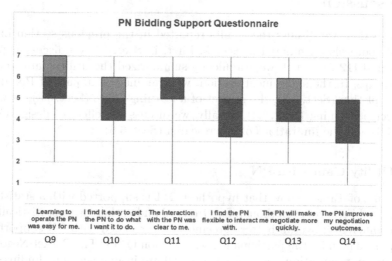

Fig. 9. Participants thoughts about the PN's bidding support

The responses of the participants on statements regarding usability and effectiveness of PN were rather positive, see Fig. 9. They found it easy to learn to operate PN, and to make it do what they want, they found the interaction clear and flexible, and thought that it makes them negotiate more quickly. The statement about PN improving their negotiation outcomes is also answered somewhat positively (see discussion above), which is in line with the actual outcomes of their negotiations, see Tables 1, and 2, 3. More details can be found in Appendix B.2.

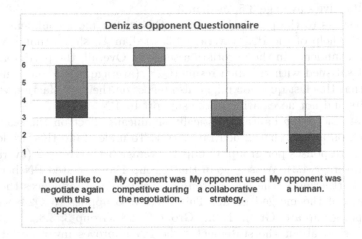

Fig. 10. Participants thoughts about Deniz agent as an opponent

6 Discussion

In this section, we discuss the results reported in the previous section in light of the hypothesis formulated in Sect. 3. First, in Sect. 6.1, we discuss hypotheses **H1** and **H2** for which we graphically summarized the utility data from the three groups. In the subsequent section, we examine the impact of PN on cognitive depletion (Sect. 6.2), the impact of a learning effect (Sect. 6.3), as well as the effect of training (Sect. 6.4). Finally, we discuss the effect of design choices (Sect. 6.5) and the limitations of our research (Sect. 6.6).

6.1 Utility Gain with PN

The results of Table 4 show that hypothesis **H1** is supported with a statistically significant difference, even though for Groups 2 and 3, there is no statistically significant difference: overall better agreements are reached with PN support. The self-reported gain by the participants, see question Q14 ("The Pocket Negotiator improves my negotiation outcomes") in Fig. 9 are in line with our findings.

We found statistically significant evidence for Hypothesis **H2:** "The utility gain for participants provided with Bidding Advice support mechanisms depends on their background." With respect to gaining utilities by getting support, we see in Table 6 and Fig. 5 that Group 1 statistically is significantly different from Group 3.

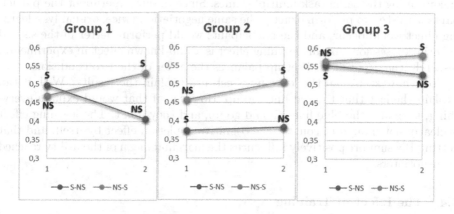

Fig. 11. Means of the utilities grouped by the start condition

Another way to study H2 is to plot the results per negotiation session. Figure 11 summarizes what happens with the marginal means of the different groups in the two conditions over two negotiation sessions, the precise data can be found in Tables 1, and 2, 3. The question is how to interpret this data. We consider two well-known effects in experimental research: cognitive depletion [1], and learning effect [18], and the influence of training and background knowledge in negotiation.

6.2 The Impact of PN on Cognitive Depletion

Cognitive depletion is the notion that performing an exhausting task can deplete a person's cognitive resources. Negotiation is a complex task as motivated in the introduction, so arguably, after completing the first negotiation session, the participants' cognitive resources are somewhat depleted so that they would not perform as well in the second negotiation.

If the cognitive depletion effect indeed holds, then what is the effect of supporting the participants in one of their negotiation sessions? If the participants benefit from the ENS, then the support should somewhat counter the cognitive depletion effect. If the participants do not benefit from the support then the cognitive depletion should be the same or worse than in the unsupported sessions. The blue lines, corresponding to the S-NS conditions, go down in Groups 1 and 3, and marginally go up in Group 2. This is in line with the cognitive depletion effect. Figure 11 shows that the red lines (corresponding to the NS-S conditions) go up in all groups. Therefore, the cognitive depletion effect is reduced by Pocket Negotiator support.

6.3 Learning Effect

The learning effect is the notion that participants learn about the task when encountering the same task multiple times. Since in our experiment the participants are asked to perform exactly the same negotiation twice, arguably, a learning effect would occur, and the participants would perform better in the second negotiation session. As this learning effect is a well-known effect in experimental research, the experimental set-up balances the order of the two conditions.

To what extent can the learning effect also explain the results? Well, it can explain the fact that the red lines go up. However, if that would explain everything, then also the blue lines should go up, and they don't. The learning effect is clearly not enough to counter the cognitive depletion effect by itself, and that getting PN support positively influences the marginal mean of the utility reached by negotiators.

6.4 The Effect of Training

The three groups differ in the background in two ways; the participants study in different studies, and they received different training and education in negotiation. In brief, Group 1 - Computer Science, with one lecture on Negotiation and ENS to prepare them, Group 2 - Industrial Engineering, with no lecture to prepare them, and Group 3 - Business Administration, with a whole course on negotiation. Both groups 1 and 3 did have only one lecture in which they were introduced to PN, which entailed showing them in 10 min how an experienced person would use it, and then having a 15 min training session within a different negotiation domain than the sessions that we base our data on. Group 2 did not get any such introduction to PN, neither on negotiation.

Based on their background, one would assume that in the No-Support conditions, the means of the utilities of the groups would show the ranking: Group 3 > Group 1 > Group 2, which is confirmed by the data, see Table 12, which takes the data from Tables 1, 2, and 3. In fact, regarding the overall means of the two sessions, the utility of Group 2 is statistically significantly lower than that of Groups 1 and 3, and similarly, the utility of Group 1 is statistically significantly lower than that of Group 3, see Table 12. One might conclude that the proficiency of Group 3 stems from their strong negotiation background (yes, education helps!).

What is the effect of PN support on this? We make the following observations: in the first negotiations, Group 1 participants do slightly better with S than without, whereas Group 2 and Group 3 participants do better without support. Definitely, Group 2 struggles with PN in the support mode. One can see an effect here between the two sessions, in that for all groups considering the participants that get support, the means of the utilities in the second sessions is higher than that in the first session (see Fig. 11). In fact, here we see that the difference

Table 12. No-support utility: means for the no-support condition for all groups. Note that there is a statistically significant difference on the overall data between Group 3 and other groups according to Mann-Whitney U test ($p < 0.5$) while there is no significant difference between Group 1 and Group 2.

Group	1st session	2nd session	Difference	Overall	Knowledge
Group 1 (CS)	0.470	0.407	−0.063	0.438	1 lecture
Group 2 (IE)	0.457	0.385	−0.072	0.421	no lecture
Group 3 (BA)	0.564	0.528	−0.036	0.544	1 course

between the utilities achieved in those sessions is bigger for Group 2 than for the other groups: Group 2 > Group 1 > Group 3, see Table 13. A potential explanation for this is that the Group 2 participants who did a negotiation without support in the first session are less confused by the support PN has to offer than the other half of Group 1 who had to master both the negotiation concept and the support given by PN in their first session. As the difference in means for Groups 1 and 3 are also positive, to some extent, the same might hold for them. The subgroups of the groups are not big enough to say anything about the statistical significance. So more research is needed to find out to what extent the learning effect of two negotiation sessions impacts the ease with which participants can use PN for the first time.

Table 13. Utility: means in the support condition for all groups. Note that there is a statistically significant difference on the overall data between Group 3 and other groups according to Mann-Whitney U test ($p < 0.5$) while there is no significant difference between Group 1 and Group 2.

Group	1st session	2nd session	Difference	Overall	Knowledge
Group 1 (CS)	0.497	0.532	0.035	0.515	1 lecture
Group 2 (IE)	0.375	0.506	0.131	0.440	no lecture
Group 3 (BA)	0.552	0.582	0.030	0.565	1 course

6.5 The Impact of Design Choices

Our literature survey revealed that not only the support mechanisms by themselves but also how they are integrated in the system plays a key role in their effectiveness. Some literature studies showed empirically that the negotiation support tool they used improves the negotiation outcome, see e.g., [2,7], while others do not, see [24]. In Sect. 3, we formulated two hypotheses on this. **H3:** The usage of passive Bidding Advice mechanisms is sub-optimal. Moreover, **H4:** Bidding Advice Mechanisms that implicitly make use of negotiation knowledge nudge the user towards more effective negotiations.

The results reported in Tables 10 and 11 provide insights regarding the usage of the passive bidding support mechanisms in PN, showing indeed that these mechanisms are not optimally used by the participants, but also that those participants that did use them had higher outcomes. Another argument for the conclusion that the support mechanisms were not optimally used is presented in Appendix C. If the participants would have clicked on the "Suggest bid" (k Best Offers mechanism with $k = 1$) in every round, and would offer that to their opponent in that round, on average they would have increased their outcome. However, in every group there were some students that achieved that utility or even more; some even managed that in the No-support version, see Table 14. None of them followed fully the Deniz-agent's strategy.

Having this result on the clickable bidding support mechanisms (k Best Offers - "Suggest bid", and Graphical Offer Selection) still leaves open the question of the impact of the active non-clickable bidding support mechanisms, i.e., the Graphical Outcome Space, Negotiation History Display, and the Critiquing Offers mechanism (the red bars for the user and for the opponent). Unfortunately, with the current version of PN we cannot trace that effect directly; we could try to indirectly measure it by looking at the results of people that use none of the clickable mechanisms and compare that with a group in the No-support conditions. Given the few people (9) who did not use any of clickable mechanisms, we leave that for future work. So, for now we conclude, that the Graphical Offer Selection mechanism had the most impact (and statistically significant positive impact at that) on the negotiation outcomes.

To what extent are the usage patterns of passive Bidding Advice mechanisms influenced by the participants' main topic of study? The BA students (Group 3) have learned about making trade-offs, about reservation values, and that careful consideration of trade-offs might mean that you can get the opponent to concede more than you initially thought possible. These insights were not present in Group 1. Both groups understand the concept of Pareto Optimality and utility. Based on these considerations, one might argue that the BA students are more carefully considering what trade-offs are made in the different bids, and the CS students might be more easily satisfied by having an outcome on the Pareto Optimal Frontier that seems more or less equal to both negotiators. For the CS students, therefore, walking the Pareto Optimal Frontier using Graphical Bid Selection might be more attractive than for BA students, see Table 7 while BA students may prefer to ask for bidding suggestions more. These observations are in support of hypothesis **H2**, which says that the utility gain depends on the background of the user.

The results of Table 5, and the participant survey responses, show that some participants followed the bid suggestions while others modified them. We observed that the EPOF accompanied with the Graphical Bid Selection mechanism is useful. It implicitly leads human negotiators to avoid suboptimal offers. Moreover, we hypothesize that the participants felt that the recommendations made by PN were sometimes too hardheaded (causing them to modify the bids), and that the Graphical Bid Selection on the EPOF makes it easier for them to make a concession that fits with their own bidding strategy. Based on those findings and observations, it is clear that there is room for improvement for which we propose the following two guidelines for the design of ENS systems for human negotiators:

- **Guideline-1**: Provide support mechanisms that actively push support, as those are more effective than passive support mechanisms.
- **Guideline-2**: Provide implicit support mechanisms that shield the user from mathematical complexities.

6.6   Limitations

As Gettinger *et al.* [9] pointed out, focusing attention primarily on the support tools may serve to distance negotiators from each other. With that in mind, one should realize that the experiments done in their work, our work, that of [4] and others that have run experiments with (parts of) ENS support mechanisms all were some sort of lab experiment; the participants were presented with a relatively simple negotiation task of our choosing in a setting that would allow us to research the potential effect of the support mechanism studied. They were not done in real negotiations, nor was the objective to find out in what ways these support mechanisms could be best deployed. This also becomes clear in how our results showed how our participants, that only had half an hour to get to know the bidding support of PN only made limited use of the various support mechanisms it offers to them. Given the insights of [9] one might speculate whether the significant improvement of the negotiation outcomes might be due to the fact that the participants were not allowed to freely interact with their counterpart, but only through the interfaces of the system. Given the complementary nature of the support mechanisms offered by the existing systems, ideally a flexible architecture for ENS would be set up in which these mechanisms can be toggled on and off and serve to provide passive or pro-active support to users in their negotiation roles, and to make this adaptive to the user's expertise and way of working.

7   Conclusions and Future Work

This paper researches the effect on utility and the extent of usage of the set of economic decision support mechanisms that can be found in the Pocket Negotiator [15]. We found evidence that the use of implicit knowledge can be beneficial for the user as it can shield the user from mathematical complexities. Finally, we found indications in the literature that the usage and effectiveness of the ENS system might well depend on the background of the user, in terms of their technical skills and negotiation skills and knowledge. The hypotheses we used in our research reflect these ideas.

To study our hypotheses, we conducted user experiments with the so-far untested bidding support mechanisms of the Pocket Negotiator (PN). The participants negotiated in two versions of PN, one with (S) and one without support

(NS) in a balanced setup over two negotiation sessions. A post-experiment questionnaire provided insight into the user experience of PN. To get insight into the impact of the background of the users, we formed three groups with different backgrounds in terms of technical skills and negotiation knowledge.

As our discussion in Sect. 6 shows, that, in general, the Pocket Negotiator improves negotiation outcomes, and that the way the passive mechanisms are used depends on the negotiation background of the participants. We found that cognitive depletion effects are countered by PN support. The implicit k Best Offers mechanism was used most effectively by the group with the most negotiation skills, but in general, was not used optimally. The implicit Graphical Offer Selection mechanism, which allows users to click on offers on the EPOF, nudges participants to make Pareto Optimal offers, which by itself already reduces the probability of "leaving money on the table". Both of these mechanisms were used in an exploratory way, and not immediately followed up in making an offer to the opponent. As expected, the participants with higher negotiation skills outperformed the other groups, but still they benefited from the support. Our experimental results show that people with enough technical skills and with some basic negotiation knowledge will benefit more from PN support than others, in that their gain in utility is higher than that of other groups.

The subjective results, based on the questionnaire, show that participants found Pocket Negotiator easy to interact with. They reported that with Pocket Negotiator they could negotiate more quickly and reach better outcomes, which was in line with their negotiation results. Furthermore, they considered the opponent to be a competitive negotiator. Based on our findings and discussion, we conclude that the current form of Pocket Negotiator is an effective tool that increases the performance of the human negotiator, but that it is a tool that users need to familiarize themselves with before they use it in practice as they did not make the most effective use of the bidding support mechanisms provided to them.

Based on our findings, we formulated two guidelines for the design of ENS systems, i.e., to make mechanisms actively push their advice to the user, and to provide implicit mechanisms to shield the user from mathematical complexities.

In terms of objective measures, we found that

- Using the Pocket Negotiator as negotiation support system increases the outcome utility of negotiation in general. This effect is statistically significant according to Wilcoxon Signed-Rank Test ($z = -3.6011$ and $p = 0.0003 < 0.05$) as shown in Table 4;
- Using the Pocket Negotiator statistically significantly increases the average number of participants bids on the EPOF as shown in Tables 7 and 9;
- When compared to the k Best Offers mechanism ("Suggest bid" in PN), the Graphical Bid Selection mechanism had the higher positive impact on the negotiation outcomes: its impact was statistically significantly different as shown in Table 10 and Table 11.

– The Bidding Advice mechanisms were not used at its most effective, as following that advice to the full would significantly improve their outcomes (see Sect. 6.5).

As usual, our research results open up new avenues for further research. For example, in the experiments for this paper, the participants received correct and complete information on the opponent's preferences, although we did not explicitly tell them so. For future research it would be interesting to study how participants deal with potentially incorrect and incomplete preference profiles and whether or not the ENS system could help them detect this. Furthermore, we realize that also the opponent bidding strategy might have an impact on our experimental results. It would be interesting to experiment with several different opponent bidding strategies, such as hardheaded, Tit-for-Tat, and random.

In general, to boost the research on support mechanisms, we should be able to measure how well people use the different support mechanisms of ENS systems. For this purpose, a method and framework has to be invented in which these mechanisms can be toggled to be included or not, toggled between passive and active, and toggle between implicit and explicit variants of the mechanism. Currently, systems are tested as a whole, which makes it difficult to assess the impact of the individual mechanisms. Such a framework would also make it possible to adapt the ENS to the needs of the user. Furthermore, in particular, bidding advice strategies should be tailored with respect to the negotiation attitude and personality of the users.

Acknowledgments. This research was (partly) funded by the https://www.hybrid-intelligence-centre.nl/,Hybrid Intelligence Center, a 10-year programme funded the Dutch Ministry of Education, Culture and Science through the Netherlands Organisation for Scientific Research, grant number 024.004.022 and by EU H2020 ICT48 project "Humane AI Net" under contract # 952026. Moreover, this work has been partially supported by the CHIST-ERA grant CHIST-ERA-19-XAI-005, and by *(i)* the Swiss National Science Foundation (G.A. 20CH21_195530), *(ii)* the Italian Ministry for Universities and Research, *(iii)* the Luxembourg National Research Fund (G.A. INTER/CHIST/19/14589586), *(iv)* the Scientific and Research Council of Turkey (TÜBİTAK, G.A. 120N680).

A   The Pocket Negotiator - Job Negotiation Description

The information on the negotiation scenario given to the participants.

Suppose you have recently conducted a successful job interview, and you are now scheduled for a contract negotiation with your potential boss. In this experiment, you will negotiate twice with your future employer, once with negotiation support, and once without.

The following issues are at stake: salary, fte (full time equivalent), work from home,lease car, permanent contract, and career development opportunities.

There are four things that drive you in general: family life, wealth, status and ambition, and team spirit. You describe yourself as follows:

I feel more comfortable if I have some job security. I have a seven-year old daughter and a new-born son. I don't need to live in wealth, but to meet their expenses, it would be great if I can agree on a high salary. Furthermore, since my partner is working on Mondays and Fridays, I need to take care of our new-born son on those days. I am an ambitious person, and I consider myself a team-player; therefore, I prefer to work full time. I also prefer a job that provides some career development opportunities, such as being able to participate in several personal development workshops, although I could do without. The office is quite some distance from my home, and I would like to make some family trips. Therefore, it would be great if the company could provide me with a lease car.

Therefore, your preferences would be like:

- Permanent contract: Yes ≻ No
- Work from home : 2 days ≻ 1day ≻ None
- Career development Opportunities: High ≻ Medium ≻ Low
- Lease car: Yes ≻ No
- Salary: 4000 ≻ 3500 ≻ 3000¿≻ 2500 ≻ 2000
- FTE: 1.0≻ 0.8 ≻ 0.6

where (value 1 ≻ value 2) means that you prefer value 1 over value 2. The ordering of the importance of those issues would be: FTE ≻ Salary ≻ Work from home ≻ Permanent Contract ≻ Lease car ≻ Career Development Opportunities where (issue 1 ≻ issue 2) means that issue 1 is more important than issue 2 for you. More details about this preference ordering can be found in Appendix 1 "My preference profile"[3].

In your first exploratory meeting with your boss, you already got to know each other a little bit. During this exploration phase, you made the following notes about your boss:

My boss owns a small company and has only a limited budget, so the main issues for him are the salary and the contract duration. I am sure he would prefer to give less salary to me if he can. He probably will not be inclined to lease a car since it would be an extra cost for him. He mentions he had some bad experiences with his former employees that he hired in the past. Although he didn't like their performance, he couldn't fire them because of their permanent contract. Furthermore, he hinted that he likes to work with small, effective teams. I asked him about career development opportunities, but he was rather vague about it.

From this information, you extract that your boss preferences would be like:

- Permanent contract: No ≻ Yes
- Work from home : None ≻ 1 day ≻ 2 days
- Career development Opportunities: Low ≻ Medium ≻ High
- Lease car: No ≻ Yes
- Salary: 2000 ≻ 2500 ≻ 3000 ≻ 3500 ≻ 4000
- FTE: 1.0 ≻ 0.8 ≻ 0.6

---

[3] The appendix mentioned here is left out for reasons of brevity and can obtained from the authors.

where (value 1 ≻ value 2) means that he prefers value 1 over value 2. The ordering of the importance of those issues would be: Work from home ≻ Permanent Contract ≻ Salary ≻ FTE ≻ Career Development Opportunities ≻ Lease car, where (issue 1 ≻ issue 2) means that issue 1 is more important than issue 2 for him. More details about the preference profile of your boss can be found in Appendix 2 "Boss profile"[4].

B Online Questionnaire

After completing the negotiation, all participants were asked to fill in an online questionnaire. The questions are renumbered and listed in Sect. B.1. We applied ANOVA all-between analysis on the responses we received from the participants, the results are presented in Sect. B.2.

B.1 List of Questions

1. Timestamp
2. What is your gender?
3. What is your age?
4. What is the highest level of education you have completed?
5. Group Type
6. Did you see the demonstration of the Pocket Negotiator before doing this experiment?
7. I am confident about my negotiation skills
8. I consider myself to be a strong negotiator.
9. Learning to operate the Pocket Negotiator was easy for me.
10. I find it easy to get the Pocket Negotiator to do what I want it to do.
11. The interaction with the Pocket Negotiator was clear to me.
12. I find the Pocket Negotiator flexible to interact with.
13. The Pocket Negotiator will make me negotiate more quickly.
14. The Pocket Negotiator improves my negotiation outcomes.
15. I could negotiate better when I had the PN support.
16. It was easier for me to negotiate when I had the PN support.
17. Without the PN support, I can concentrate better.
18. The negotiation outcome was better when I had the PN support.
19. Without the PN support, we found an agreement sooner.
20. I had a better understanding of what is going on during the negotiation when I had the PN support.
21. Using the Pocket Negotiator made it harder to find good agreements.
22. I could gain a better agreement without the PN support.
23. I found the PN distracted me from the negotiation.
24. I felt more confident negotiating with the help of the PN
25. The bids I made using the PN were more self-serving.

---

[4] Also this appendix is left out for reasons of brevity and can obtained from the authors.

26. The PN made it harder for me to pursue my own interests.
27. In the exercises without the PN, I frequently made complete bids.
28. I am satisfied with the end result.
29. I made the bids as suggested by the PN.
30. I modified the bids as suggested by the PN.
31. I would concede more than the PN advises.
32. I found the predefined bids on the line in the picture useful.
33. I would like to negotiate again with this opponent sometime in the future.
34. I took my opponent's preferences into account during the negotiation.
35. I took my own preferences into account during the negotiation.
36. I took my opponent's strategy into account while deciding my next move.
37. I adopted a collaborative negotiation strategy.
38. I was competitive during the negotiation.
39. My opponent was competitive during the negotiation.
40. My opponent used a collaborative strategy.
41. My opponent was a human.

B.2   ANOVA analyis of the Questionnaire Results

- "The Pocket Negotiator improves my negotiation outcomes.": Group has a significant difference (p value = 0.014; Fratio = 4.7 and dF = 2);
- "It was easier for me to negotiate when I had the PN support.": Group has a significant difference (p value = 0.002; Fratio = 6.8 and dF = 2) and age, group and sawdemo (p value = 0.036; Fratio = 4.6 and dF = 1).
- "I could gain a better agreement without the PN support.": Group has a significant difference (p value = 0.012; Fratio = 4.8 and dF = 2).
- "I found the PN distracted me from the negotiation.": Group has a significant difference (p value = 0.032; Fratio = 3.7 and dF = 2).
- "I am satisfied with the end results.": age and education have a significant difference (p value = 0.008; Fratio = 7.5 and dF = 1) and education and group (p value = 0.018; Fratio = 4.5 and dF = 2).
- "I would concede more than the PN advices.": Group has a significant difference (p value = 0.021; Fratio = 4.2 and dF = 2).
- "I found the predefined bids on the line in the picture useful.": Group has a significant difference (p value = 0.007; Fratio = 5.4 and dF = 2).
- "I would like to negotiate again with this opponent sometime in the future."; Age has a significant difference (p value = 0.021; Fratio = 5.6 and dF = 1) and group (p value = 0.017; Fratio = 4.4 and dF = 2).
- "I took my opponent's preferences into account during the negotiation.": Education has a significant difference (p value = 0.029; Fratio = 3.8 and dF =2).
- "I took my own preferences into account during the negotiation.": Group has a significant difference (p value = 0.042; Fratio =3.4 and dF =2) and age and sawdemo (p value = 0.038; Fratio = 4.5 and dF = 1).
- "I took my opponent's strategy into account while deciding my next move). Group and sawdemo have a significant difference (p value=0.014; Fratio=4.7 and dF=2).

- "I adopted a collaborative negotiation strategy.": Age has a significant difference (p value = 0.001; Fratio =11.4 and dF=1) and education and group (p value=0.018; fRatio = 4.3 dF = 2);
- "My opponent was using a collaborative strategy": Group has a significant difference (p value = 0.006; Fratio = 5.6 and dF = 2).

C   Self-Play in PN and Individual Outcomes

The subjects in our experiments were negotiating against a software agent, called Deniz [14], and that a copy of Deniz supported the participants. This means that if the subjects would follow the recommendation exactly, the Deniz agent would negotiate with itself. However, none of our human participants that did that.

Table 14 shows the number of participants who achieved an outcome with a utility that was at least as high as Deniz agent would have achieved when playing against itself (Utility = 0.58).

Table 14. The number of participants who received at least as high utility as Deniz agent received when it plays against itself

Group	S in session 1	NS in session 1	S in session 2	NS in session 2
Group 1	–	–	2 (0.61;0.69)	–
Group 2	–	1 (0.70)	1 (0.76)	1 (0.59)
Group 3	4 (0.59–0.72)	7 (0.58–0.72)	9 (0.58–0.72)	3 (0.61–0.67)

In our experiments, the Bidding Advice mechanism is actually hardly asked for, and the advice is not always follow-up by the participants, as we reported as one of our findings. So there is no self-play in the experiment. Furthermore, the Deniz agent does not know what strategy the other is playing (neither as supporting agent, nor as opponent agent) and has no mechanisms for manipulating such foreknowledge, see [14], where the results of Deniz's self-play are reported.

We could have let the participants play against multiple opponents however, we think one should first make sure that participants use support mechanisms of the agent more often and more effectively. After that, of course, more elaborate experiments are in order, with more agents, and many more negotiation scenarios (from 1 to many negotiation issues, with issue inter-dependencies and without).

References

1. Baumeister, R.F., Vohs, K.D., Tice, D.M.: The strength model of self-control. Curr. Dir. Psychol. Sci. **16**(6), 351–355 (2007)
2. Bosse, T., Jonker, C.M.: Human vs. computer behavior in multi-issue negotiation. In: Rational, Robust, and Secure Negotiation Mechanisms in Multi-Agent Systems (RRS'05), pp. 11–24. IEEE (2005)

3. Broekens, J., Harbers, M., Brinkman, W.-P., Jonker, C.M., Van den Bosch, K., Meyer, J.-J.: Virtual reality negotiation training increases negotiation knowledge and skill. In: Nakano, Y., Neff, M., Paiva, A., Walker, M. (eds.) IVA 2012. LNCS (LNAI), vol. 7502, pp. 218–230. Springer, Heidelberg (2012). https://doi.org/10. 1007/978-3-642-33197-8_23
4. Chen, E., Vahidov, R., Kersten, G.E.: Agent-supported negotiations in the e-marketplace. Int. J. Electron. Bus. **3**(1), 28–49 (2005)
5. Fisher, R., William, L.: Getting to Yes. Penguin Group, New York (1981)
6. Foroughi, A., Perkins, W., Jelassi, T.: An empirical study of an interactive, session-oriented computerized negotiation support system (NSS). Group Decis. Negotiat. **4**, 485–512 (1995). 10.1007/BF01409712
7. Foroughi, A., Perkins, W.C., Hershauer, J.C.: A study of asymmetrical decision support in computerized negotiation support systems (NSS). Glob. Bus. Fin. Rev. (GBFR) **20**(1), 25–42 (2015)
8. G., K., Lai, H.: Negotiation support and e-negotiation systems: an overview. Group Decis. Negot. **16**, 553—586 (2007)
9. Gettinger, J., et al.: Impact of and interaction between behavioral and economic decision support in electronic negotiations. In: Hernández, J.E., Zarate, P., Dargam, F., Delibašić, B., Liu, S., Ribeiro, R. (eds.) EWG-DSS 2011. LNBIP, vol. 121, pp. 151–165. Springer, Heidelberg (2012). https://doi.org/10.1007/978-3-642-32191-7_11
10. Gratch, J., DeVault, D., Lucas, G.: The benefits of virtual humans for teaching negotiation. In: Traum, D., Swartout, W., Khooshabeh, P., Kopp, S., Scherer, S., Leuski, A. (eds.) IVA 2016. LNCS (LNAI), vol. 10011, pp. 283–294. Springer, Cham (2016). https://doi.org/10.1007/978-3-319-47665-0_25
11. Gratch, J., Nazari, Z., Johnson, E.: The misrepresentation game: how to win at negotiation while seeming like a nice guy. In: Proceedings of the 2016 International Conference on Autonomous Agents & Multiagent Systems, pp. 728–737. IFAAMAS (2016)
12. Hindriks, K., Tykhonov, D.: Opponent modelling in automated multi-issue negotiation using Bayesian learning. In: Proceedings of the 7th International Joint Conference on Autonomous Agents and Multiagent Systems-vol. 1. pp. 331–338. International Foundation for Autonomous Agents and Multiagent Systems (2008)
13. Jonker, C.M., et al.: An introduction to the pocket negotiator: a general purpose negotiation support system. In: Criado Pacheco, N., Carrascosa, C., Osman, N., Julián Inglada, V. (eds.) EUMAS/AT -2016. LNCS (LNAI), vol. 10207, pp. 13–27. Springer, Cham (2017). https://doi.org/10.1007/978-3-319-59294-7_2
14. Jonker, C.M., Aydoğan, R.: Deniz: a robust bidding strategy for negotiation support systems. In: Ito, T., Zhang, M., Aydoğan, R. (eds.) ACAN 2018. SCI, vol. 905, pp. 29–44. Springer, Singapore (2021). https://doi.org/10.1007/978-981-15-5869-6_3
15. Jonker, C.M., et al.: An introduction to the pocket negotiator: a general purpose negotiation support system. In: Criado Pacheco, N., Carrascosa, C., Osman, N., Julián Inglada, V. (eds.) EUMAS/AT -2016. LNCS (LNAI), vol. 10207, pp. 13–27. Springer, Cham (2017). https://doi.org/10.1007/978-3-319-59294-7_2
16. Jonker, C.M., Aydoğan, R., Baarslag, T., Fujita, K., Ito, T., Hindriks, K.V.: Automated negotiating agents competition (ANAC). In: AAAI, pp. 5070–5072 (2017)
17. van Krimpen, T., Looije, D., Hajizadeh, S.: Hardheaded. In: Ito, T., Zhang, M., Robu, V., Matsuo, T. (eds) Complex Automated Negotiations: Theories, Models, and Software Competitions, vol. 435, pp. 223–227. Springer, Heidelberg (2013). https://doi.org/10.1007/978-3-642-30737-9_17

18. Lazar, J., Feng, L.H., Hochheiser, H.: Research Methods in Human-Computer Interaction. Willey, Chichester (2010)
19. Lewicki, R.J., Saunders, D.M., Barry, B., Minton, J.W.: Essentials of Negotiation. McGraw-Hill, Boston (2003)
20. Mell, J., Gratch, J., Baarslag, T., Aydoğan, R., Jonker, C.M.: Results of the first annual human-agent league of the automated negotiating agents competition. In: Proceedings of the 18th International Conference on Intelligent Virtual Agents, pp. 23–28. IVA '18, ACM, New York, NY, USA (2018). 10.1145/3267851.3267907, http://doi.acm.org/10.1145/3267851.3267907
21. de Melo, C.M., Marsella, S., Gratch, J.: Do as I say, not as I do: challenges in delegating decisions to automated agents. In: Proceedings of the 2016 International Conference on Autonomous Agents & Multiagent Systems, pp. 949–956. IFAAMAS (2016)
22. Raiffa, H.: The Art and Science of Negotiation. Belknap Press, reprint edn. (2005), first version from 1982
23. Raiffa, H., Richardson, J., Metcalfe, D.: Negotiation Analysis: The Science and Art of Collaborative Decision Making (2002)
24. Schoop, M., van Amelsvoort, M., Gettinger, J., Koerner, M., Koeszegi, S.T., van der Wijst, P.: The interplay of communication and decisions in electronic negotiations: communicative decisions or decisive communication? Group Decis. Negot. 23(2), 167–192 (2014)
25. Thompson, L.: The Mind and Heart of the Negotiator, 3rd edn. Prentice Hall Press, Upper Saddle River (2000)
26. Yuasa, M., Yasumura, Y., Nitta, K.: A negotiation support tool using emotional factors. In: Proceedings Joint 9th IFSA World Congress and 20th NAFIPS International Conference (Cat. No. 01TH8569), pp. 2906–2911. IEEE (2001)

Automated Negotiating Agent Competition

The 13th International Automated Negotiating Agent Competition Challenges and Results

Reyhan Aydoğan[1,2](✉)(iD), Tim Baarslag[3,4], Katsuhide Fujita[5,6](iD),
Holger H. Hoos[7,8,9], Catholijn M. Jonker[2,8], Yasser Mohammad[6,10],
and Bram M. Renting[2,8]

[1] Özyeğin University, Computer Science, Istanbul, Turkey
reyhan.aydogan@ozyegin.edu.tr
[2] Delft University of Technology, Interactive Intelligence Group, Delft,
The Netherlands
c.m.jonker@tudelft.nl
[3] Centrum Wiskunde and Informatica, Amsterdam, The Netherlands
T.Baarslag@cwi.nl
[4] Utrecht University, Utrecht, The Netherlands
[5] Tokyo University of Agriculture and Technology,
Tokyo, Japan
katfuji@cc.tuat.ac.jp
[6] National Institute of Advanced Industrial Science and Technology (AIST),
Tokyo, Japan
[7] RWTH Aachen University, Aachen, Germany
hh@aim.rwth-aachen.de
[8] Leiden University, Leiden, The Netherlands
B.M.Renting@liacs.leidenuniv.nl
[9] University of British Columbia, Vancouver, Canada
[10] NEC Corporation, Tokyo, Japan

Abstract. An international competition for negotiating agents has been organized for years to facilitate research in agent-based negotiation and to encourage the design of negotiating agents that can operate in various scenarios. The 13th International Automated Negotiating Agents Competition (ANAC 2022) was held in conjunction with IJCAI2022. In ANAC2022, we had two leagues: Automated Negotiation League (ANL) and Supply Chain Management League (SCML). For the ANL, the participants designed a negotiation agent that can learn from the previous bilateral negotiation sessions it was involved in. In contrast, the research challenge was to make the right decisions to maximize the overall profit in a supply chain environment, such as determining with whom and when to negotiate. This chapter describes the overview of ANL and SCML in ANAC2022, and reports the results of each league, respectively.

© The Author(s), under exclusive license to Springer Nature Singapore Pte Ltd. 2023
R. Hadfi et al. (Eds.): IJCAI 2022, SCI 1092, pp. 87–101, 2023.
https://doi.org/10.1007/978-981-99-0561-4_5

1 Introduction

Negotiation is one of the processes aiming to form alliances and find mutually acceptable solutions when stakeholders have conflicts of interest or objectives. It can be considered as a search problem in which we are looking for a decision that the majority/all stakeholders are pleased with. Research in the field of negotiation originates from various disciplines, including economics, social sciences, game theory, and artificial intelligence. The artificial intelligence community focuses on designing and developing negotiating agents that can automatically negotiate with their partners. That requires understanding the negotiation problem, reasoning on the given objectives and preferences, making strategic decisions leading to profitable consequences, and adapting behaviour based on their opponent's moves and environmental conditions such as remaining negotiation time. At this point, the International Automated Negotiating Agents Competition (ANAC) plays a vital role in developing effective negotiation strategies and providing a benchmark for the community. Consequently, the organizers of this competition aimed to encourage the design of agents that can negotiate proficiently in various circumstances and objectively assess the performance of different bargaining strategies designed by researchers worldwide. In addition, we aim to collect and make available state-of-the-art negotiating agents, negotiation domains, and preference profiles for the negotiation research community.

ANAC has studied various negotiation problems and research challenges in this field since its inception in 2010 [5]. It has focused on bilateral negotiations with reservation values and discount factors [4,5,12], large and varying domains [7,13], multilateral and non-linear settings [6], and repeated [2] negotiations. Since 2017, ANAC has had different leagues with their own challenges. In 2022, the two leagues were set up as follows:

- **Automated Negotiation League (ANL)**: Designing a negotiation agent for bilateral negotiation that can learn from previous encounters while the tournament progresses.
- **Supply Chain Management League (SCML)** [9]: Designing factory agents aiming to maximize their profit in a competitive market environment. Therefore, agents must decide with whom and when to negotiate to get the necessary sources to produce their products which will be sold to the end customers.

In negotiation, there are a variety of research challenges spanning from reasoning on incomplete information to learning about the opponent's preferences or strategies and adapting behaviour accordingly. In previous years of ANL, we introduced the challenge of learning across negotiation sessions which took much attention from our participants; however, the setting had some limitations due to the framework constraints and security concerns. The framework allowed agents to store only some structured data from their previous negotiation sessions, such as the utility distribution of their offer exchanges. However, agents may use other types of information to get a better deal. This year, agents can store any information from their previous negotiation sessions and utilize the learned knowledge in their subsequent negotiations. Regarding the SCML, the problem description and challenges were too complicated to deal with; therefore, this year, the rules were mainly simplified to streamline the challenges of maximizing profit by negotiating trades with other agents simultaneously. Consequently, agent designers could focus on one particular challenge.

The remainder of this chapter is organized as follows. Section 2 provides an overview of ANL in ANAC2022. In Sect. 3, we present the setup of SCML in ANAC2022. Section 4 discusses the results of ANL and SCML, respectively. Finally, Sect. 5 outlines our conclusions and plans for future competitions.

2 Automated Negotiation League

The Automated Negotiating Agents Competition (ANAC) originally consisted of a single challenge [3]. Since 2017, new challenges have been added, and the original competition was renamed to the Automated Negotiation League (ANL). The ANL is focused purely on the development of negotiation strategies for agents negotiating with other agents, where each year, a specific challenge is introduced by the organizers. We start by laying out the background knowledge before introducing the 2022 challenge and evaluation method. The competition results will be discussed in Sect. 4.1.

2.1 Background

In ANL, we focus on bilateral negotiations where two agents negotiate on a particular scenario to reach a consensus. Agents exchange offers by following the Alternating Offers Protocol (AOP) [1,11], where agents take turns having three possible actions: making a (counter) offer, accepting the previous offer, or walking away from the negotiation. Usually, a deadline is used to prevent agents from negotiating indefinitely, and in ANL 2022, we have set a deadline of 60 s in wall-clock time. Agents must reach an agreement before the deadline passes. Failing to reach an agreement results in a reservation utility, mostly a utility of zero, for both agents involved.

2.2 Negotiation Problem

The negotiation problem, also known as the negotiation domain, defines the set of negotiation issues and their possible values, the space Ω in which an outcome $\omega \in \Omega$ of the negotiation must be agreed upon by the agents. Such a domain generally consists of a set of sub-problems or issues $I \in \mathcal{I}$; for instance, when negotiating over buying new computing facilities, not only the price is important, but also delivery times, hardware specs, brand, installation costs, etc. In this league, we make the simplifying assumption that all the issues are discrete. For each issue, there is thus a fixed set of values $I = \{v_1, \cdots, v_k\}$. The Cartesian product of all the issues comprises the outcome space $\Omega = I_1 \times \cdots \times I_n$ of the negotiation. The agents try to agree upon an outcome $\omega = (\omega_1, \omega_2, \cdots, \omega_n) \in \Omega$, where n is the cardinality of the set of issues, and $\omega_i \in I_i$.

The agents have preferences over the outcome space that are considered private information. Their preferences are represented through a utility function that maps an outcome to a value $u : \Omega \to [0,1]$, where 1 is the utility value that the agent can get in case of reaching the best possible outcome. In this league, we use linear additive utility functions, in which each issue I_i has an associated weight w_i, where $\sum_{i=1}^{n} w_i = 1$. The preference over the values within an issue is expressed through the value function $v : I \mapsto [0,1]$. The overall utility of an outcome is calculated by the utility function given in Eq. 1.

$$u(\boldsymbol{\omega}) = \sum_{i=1}^{n} w_i \cdot v_i(\omega_i) \tag{1}$$

The negotiation domain and preferences, expressed by utility functions, are randomly generated. That is, we generated negotiation domains that have between 4–10 issues and have a size between 200–10 000. The preferences over the negotiation problem are also generated randomly. The code that produced the negotiation scenarios can be found in the public repository at[1].

2.3   Challenge

Each agent submitted to the league competed against each other agent in bilateral negotiation setups. Every opponent was encountered 50 times in succession on a randomly generated negotiation scenario. The results were averaged and sorted based on two evaluation criteria: *individual utility*, and *social welfare*. Social welfare is measured by the sum of the utilities of both agents involved in a negotiation and is a more social measure compared to individual utility.

What made the 2022 edition of ANL special is that participants were challenged to learn during the course of the tournament. All agents were provided with a storage location, where they could save any data they wanted, in order to deal more effectively with repeated encounters with the same opponents. In a real-world case, we might find ourselves negotiating with the same partners in, e.g. calendar scheduling scenarios or smart-grid energy trading. As we do, agents can exploit their previous experiences in their current negotiations to find better deals.

2.4   Method

As previously mentioned, every submitted agent competed against each other on 50 randomly created negotiation scenarios in succession. This succession is essential, as agents need to be able to learn from previous encounters with opponents. However, running every negotiation session in this tournament in succession is intractable, as a single tournament with 19 submitted agents would require 8550 negotiation sessions. Considering the deadline, this would have led to an upper bound of approximately 6 days in negotiation time. As explained later, multiple repetitions of the tournament needed to be run, which would have further increased the computational effort.

We opted to let every submitted agent negotiate against each other in parallel. A new round is started only when all previous sessions are finished, and we

---

[1] https://github.com/brenting/ANL-2022-example-agent.

repeat this 50 times. This ensures that a single opponent is never negotiated multiple times simultaneously and that all agents have comparable knowledge about the tournament at the start of a new round. An illustration of this procedure is given in Fig. 1.

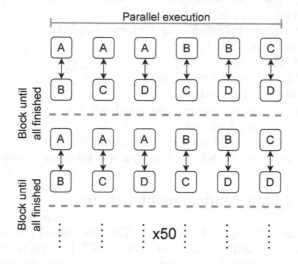

Fig. 1. Run schedule for a tournament with 4 agents: $\{A, B, C, D\}$

Negotiation scenarios were randomly generated causing a stochastic influence. Preferences can be skewed in favour of one of the agents, and the maximum obtainable social welfare can be lower for some problems. To fix the potentially skewed preferences, we repeated the tournament once more, while changing sides on the negotiation scenario by switching the utility functions. We made sure to wipe the data storage of all agents before doing so, in order to prevent unfair advantages. Furthermore, we reduced the stochastic influence by repeating the entire tournament 5 times. A total of 85,500 negotiation sessions were run to obtain the results of this competition.

2.5 Submissions

In total, there were 19 valid submissions; code and reports submitted by the participants are available online[2]. We provide an overview of the agents submitted to ANL 2022 as follows:

- Agent007, Bar Ilan University
- Agent4410, College of Management Academic Studies
- AgentFish, Tokyo University of Agriculture and Technology
- AgentFO2, Tokyo University of Agriculture and Technology

---

[2] https://tracinsy.ewi.tudelft.nl/pubtrac/GeniusWebThirdParties/browser/ANL2022.

- BIU_agent, Bar Ilan University
- ChargingBoul, University of Tulsa
- CompromisingAgent, Bar Ilan University
- DreamTeam109Agent, College of Management Academic Studies
- GEAAgent, College of Management Academic Studies
- LearningAgent, Bar Ilan University
- LuckyAgent2022, Babol Noshirvani University of Technology
- MiCROAgent, IIIA-CSIC
- Pinar_Agent, Siemens
- ProcrastinAgent, University of Tulsa
- RGAgent, Bar Ilan University
- SmartAgent, College of Management Academic Studies
- SuperAgent, Bar Ilan University
- ThirdAgent, College of Management Academic Studies
- Tjaronchery10Agent, College of Management Academic Studies.

3   Supply-Chain Management League

The Supply Chain Management League (SCML hereafter) has been one of the ANAC leagues since 2019. The main goal of SCML is to provide a realistic business-like environment for developing and evaluating negotiation strategies situated in a dynamic environment. The *SCM world* simulates a supply chain consisting of multiple factories that buy and sell products from one another. The factories are represented by autonomous agents that act as factory managers. Each agent decides which other agents to buy and sell from, and then negotiates with them. Their goal is to turn a profit, and the agent with the highest profit (averaged over multiple simulations) wins.

The simulation proceeds in discrete time steps, which we refer to as days. During each day, multiple simultaneous negotiations transpire, and outputs are manufactured from inputs. The game is intended to further research on agent negotiation; as such, the design emphasizes negotiation and de-emphasizes operations (e.g., scheduling). *Factories* in the SCM world convert *products* into other products by running *manufacturing processes* on their *production lines*. All processes take one day to complete. Factories store the inputs and outputs of manufacturing processes in their *inventories*, and their funds in their *accounts*.

Each factory has multiple production lines, each of which is assigned a profile specifying the cost at which it can execute the various manufacturing processes. In general, these costs can vary from factory to factory and may vary from line to line. Prior to SCML 2022, however, each factory had a set of identical production lines, each of which can run only a single manufacturing process. Factory costs are private information: i.e., no factory manager knows the cost of any other factory.

The production graph is assumed to be directed and acyclic, with products and manufacturing processes as its nodes. An edge from a product to a process node indicates that this product is an *input* to this process. An edge from a process to a product node indicates that this product is an *output* of this process. (Note that there are no edges between product nodes or between process nodes.) Figure 2 depicts a sample production graph for the game.

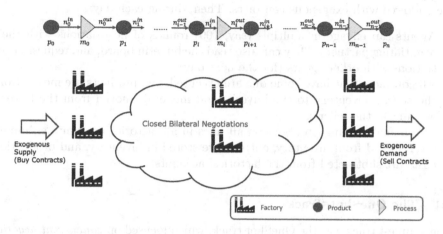

Fig. 2. Example of a world in SCML showing the production graph (top). Demand and supply are controlled through exogenous contracts while all trade in non-terminal products is conducted through closed concurrent bilateral negotiations

The agents in the SCM world function as *factory managers*. In addition to managing production, they negotiate with other agents to reach agreements to buy and sell products. Such agreements are generated via bilateral negotiations using the *alternating offers protocol* typically used in ANAC competitions [8,9]. Each offer specifies a buyer, a seller, a product, a quantity, a delivery time, and a unit price. The sequences of offers and counteroffers in a negotiation are private to the negotiating parties.

The SCM world does not endow agents with arbitrary utility functions[3]. On the contrary, all utility functions are endogenous, meaning they are engendered by the simulation dynamics and agents' interactions with other agents. Endogenous utility functions are a distinguishing feature of SCML. It is an agent's job to assign utilities to potential contracts, given its unique production capabilities, and then to negotiate with other agents to secure those which are most favorable to them.

Agents consuming raw materials are endowed with exogenous buy contracts but no exogenous sell contracts, while agents producing the finished product will be endowed with exogenous sell contracts but no exogenous buy contracts. No other agents will be endowed with any exogenous contracts. By design, *no agent can turn a profit without negotiating successfully*, since no agent is endowed with both exogenous buy and exogenous sell contracts. SCML had three tracks with gradually increasing difficulty.

---

[3] See the three tracks later for more information about this point.

Each simulation of the SCM world runs for multiple (say, 1000) days. Before the first day, each agent is assigned a *private* manufacturing profile. In addition, the bulletin board is populated with the production graph information and catalog prices, an initial balance is deposited into each agent's account, and agents are endowed with exogenous contracts. Then, during each day:

1. Agents can engage in multiple (say, 100) rounds of negotiations with their negotiating partners. They can also read the bulletin board, and request negotiations with other agents (for the next day).
2. All contracts that have come due are executed: i.e., products are moved from the seller's inventory to the buyer's, and money is moved from the buyer's account to the seller's.
3. The manufacturing processes on all lines in all factories are run: i.e., inputs are removed from inventory, outputs are stored in inventory, and production costs are subtracted from the factories' accounts.

3.1   The OneShot Track

The simplest track was the OneShot track, which focused on *concurrent negotiation* with a well-defined utility function that is given to the participants. In this track, the production graph had exactly three products (i.e. two manufacturing processes). Agents could either be on the buying end or the selling end of all their negotiations, but not both[4]. All products in OneShot are perishable (i.e., no inventory is carried over to the next day), and agents start with an initial endowment of money that guarantees that they can never go bankrupt. Exogenous contracts are revealed day by day. Moreover, all buyer agents negotiate with all seller agents every day, and all agreements reached are immediately binding (i.e., no separate signing step) and agents can—in principle—get all their needs from a single supplier (or sell all their products to a single consumer). Taken together, these features guarantee that the profit for a day is completely independent of what happened in the past or what will happen in the future given the agreements of that day and makes the utility function (profit) easy to define.

Utility Function. Agent a's utility u_a can now be defined as a's profits, i.e., its revenue less its costs and penalties:

$$
u_a(C_a^{\text{in}}, C_a^{\text{out}}) = \underbrace{\sum_{c \in C_a^{*\text{out}}} p_c q_c^{*\text{out}} - \sum_{c \in C_a^{\text{in}}} p_c q_c^{\text{in}} - m_a Q^{*\text{out}}}_{\text{revenue} \qquad\qquad \text{costs}}
$$
$$
- \underbrace{\left(\alpha_a \operatorname{tp}(\rho_a^{\text{in}}, d) Q_a^{\text{excess}} + \beta_a \operatorname{tp}(\rho_a^{\text{out}}, d) Q_a^{\text{shortfall}} \right)}_{\text{total penalties}},
$$

$$(2)$$

---

[4] Each submitted strategy was played in both roles.

where ρ_a^{in} and ρ_a^{out} are factory a's input and output products, respectively, and $\text{tp}(\rho, d)$ is the **trading price** of product ρ on day d which is a weighted average of previous actual trading prices of the product.

$\sum_{c \in C_a^{*\text{out}}} p_c q_c^{*\text{out}}$ The total **revenue** it earns by selling its outputs.

$\sum_{c \in C_a^{\text{in}}} p_c q_c^{\text{in}}$ The total **cost** it incurs to buy its inputs.

$m_a Q_a^{*\text{out}}$ The production **cost**. Note that factories produce exactly what they can sell on the current day, as inventory does not carry over from one day to the next.

$\alpha_a \, \text{tp}(\rho_a^{\text{in}}, d) \, Q_a^{\text{excess}}$ The total buy-side **penalty**, which is incurred on any output products that are not sold. Note that these penalties depend on the trading price of the input product.

$\beta_a \, \text{tp}(\rho_a^{\text{out}}, d) \, Q_a^{\text{shortfall}}$ The total sell-side **penalty** incurred by the factory for failing to deliver its output product. Note that these penalties depend on the trading price of the output product.

3.2 The Standard Track

In the standard track, products do not perish (i.e., the inventory is carried to the next day), exogenous contracts are revealed days before their due, and negotiators can reach agreements about deliveries any day in the future. Agreements are only binding once signed at the end of each day. Agents can commit breaches and may go bankrupt.

There are several challenges here. Firstly, the agent needs to take into account not only the current set of concurrently running negotiations but also future negotiations. Secondly, the agent negotiates with its suppliers and consumers concurrently. Thirdly, exogenous contracts are not forced, and agreements are not binding until they are *signed* by the end of the day. This entails that an agent cannot be sure that an agreement it has will actually be signed and must model the signing probability of its agreements. Fourthly, the agent directly controls production and must decide what to produce. Fifthly, agents may go bankrupt, affecting other agents with whom they signed contracts (like in the real world), and this actually happens frequently enough that agents should not ignore it. Finally, it is not possible to know the profit of a set of contracts on the day they are signed (as with the OneShot track), which means that each agent has to define its own – uncertain – utility function.

Breach Processing: When a contract comes due, the simulator tries to execute it (i.e., move products from the seller's inventory to the buyer's, and move money from the buyer's account to the seller's). If this execution fails, either because of insufficient funds on the part of the buyer, or insufficient products on the part of the seller, a breach of contract occurs. In both cases, the contract is executed to the extent possible, and the agent in breach of contract is penalized and reported to the breach list.

Bankruptcy Processing: If an agent is unable to meet its financial obligations, it is declared bankrupt. The assets of bankrupt agents are liquidated, and their factories are closed (no further production can transpire). They can no longer participate in negotiations. The simulator takes over their outstanding contracts and fulfils them to the extent possible.

The Spot Market: exists so that agents who would otherwise be in breach of contract for insufficient products (funds) can instead buy (sell) as necessary on the spot market at buy (sell) prices, which are always above (below) *trading prices*—an average over the historic prices at which products are traded.

3.3 The Collusion Track

In the Standard and OneShot tracks, at most one instance of each team's agent runs in each simulation, together with an unknown mix of agents prepared by other participants and agents prepared by the organizing committee. In the *collusion* track, multiple instances of the same team's agent run during a single simulation. In this track, it is perfectly legal for instances of the same agent to collude with one another to try to corner the market or exhibit other collusive behaviours. This is the main challenge added by the collusion track.

3.4 Competition Mechanics

The competition was conducted in two main phases: (1) an online phase, in which agents could be submitted to https://scml.cs.brown.edu and were automatically checked for being runnable within the simulation environment then entered into tournaments with other submitted agents with a leaderboard that is kept up to near the submission deadline for the official competition. (2) the official competition phase, which is further divided into a qualification and finals. Only top-performing agents in the qualifications were allowed to run in the finals.

For both rounds of the competition, we applied a factorial t-test (i.e., t-tests between every pair of agents) with Bonferroni's multiple comparison correction and considered two agents to have different ranks only if the differences between their scores were statistically significant.

We received a total of 76 registrations for the online competition, of which only 25 agents were submitted to the official competition; of these, 13 were selected as finalists in the three tracks (OneShot: 8, Standard: 3, Collusion: 2). Moreover, the winning agents from last year with no updated strategy this year were automatically entered into the official competition (OneShot: 2, Standard: 1). Because we only had 2 submissions in the Collusion track, both agents qualified automatically for the finals.

4 Competition Results

In this section, we first report the results of the ANL (Sect. 4.1), then present the results of the SCML (Sect. 4.2).

4.1 Automated Negotiation League Results

We present the winners of ANL 2022 in Table 1. Full results of the tournament can be found in Table 2. Surprisingly, "DreamTeam109Agent" won in both the individual utility and the social welfare categories. Optimising for individual utility generally hurts social welfare [10], but it seems that this did not prevent the agent from obtaining the highest score in both categories. The first and second places in individual utilities are close, but there is quite a significant gap between the second and third places. The difference in social welfare score between "Agent007" and "CompromisingAgent" was almost negligibly in favour of "Agent007", resulting in a close third position of the latter in terms of social welfare. Lastly, "LuckyAgent2022" had a bug in its learning mechanism, which caused it to obtain a low ranking.

Table 1. Winners of the Automated Negotiation League (ANL)

Rank	Individual utility	Social welfare
1st	DreamTeam109Agent	DreamTeam109Agent
2nd	ChargingBoul	Agent007

4.2 Supply-Chain Negotiation Results

Table 3 shows the results of the OneShot track. All qualified agents could outperform the top agents from SCML 2021, showing progress in solving the challenge. Moreover, all qualified agents except AdamAGent and EveAgent could achieve some profit (i.e. a score higher than 10, 000), with the top strategy (Patient-Agent) achieving 12.2% profit[5]. The OneShot track was run twice (once with the winners from SCML2021 and once without them). Table 3 shows that agent ranks did not change in the two runs. Moreover, removing the weakest agents did improve the profit of all other agents in the environment. The winner of this track was PatientAgent from Brown University. The three winner agents could achieve positive profits in both runs of the finals.

Table 4 shows the results of the Standard track. All newly qualified agents could outperform the second-place agent from last year (ArtisanKangaroo)[6]. Only the winner of the qualifications round (Lobster) could make a profit in this more challenging environment, and it only made 0.72%. No agents in the standard track could generate positive profits suggesting, that the challenge is still too hard for the methods explored so far. The winner agent for this track was Lobster, from Nagoya Institute of Technology, Japan that also won the qualifications.

---

[5] The simulations were designed so that a beneficial dictator optimizing agreements can achieve a 15% profit.

[6] The top agent from SCML2021 was modified and resubmitted to SCML2022 as M5.

Table 2. Results from the Automated Negotiation League (ANL), where **bold** is best and <u>underline</u> is worst. The measures are averaged over all the negotiation sessions that agents participated in.

Agent	Individual utility	Opponent utility	Nash product	Social welfare	Number of offers	Agreement ratio
DreamTeam109Agent	**0.725**	0.736	0.541	**1.460**	**6459**	0.943
ChargingBoul	0.724	0.670	0.551	1.393	5705	0.866
SuperAgent	0.704	0.576	0.505	1.280	6173	0.791
CompromisingAgent	0.686	0.771	0.550	1.456	1233	0.925
RGAgent	0.682	0.713	**0.567**	1.395	1209	0.850
LearningAgent	0.668	0.535	0.481	1.203	1272	0.733
Agent007	0.642	0.814	0.527	1.456	2554	0.956
AgentFO2	0.641	0.727	0.543	1.367	3244	0.851
ProcrastinAgent	0.640	0.376	0.357	1.016	5302	0.665
MiCROAgent	0.627	0.502	0.453	1.130	6144	0.696
Pinar_Agent	0.618	0.517	0.456	1.136	5303	0.702
BIU_agent	0.608	0.526	0.463	1.133	1422	0.685
ThirdAgent	0.591	0.721	0.508	1.313	963	0.833
Agent4410	0.581	0.818	0.514	1.399	1190	0.907
Tjaronchery10Agent	0.578	0.509	0.418	1.087	848	0.682
GEAAgent	0.576	0.727	0.505	1.303	<u>45</u>	0.826
AgentFish	0.569	**0.871**	0.507	1.440	2380	**0.957**
SmartAgent	0.553	0.356	0.339	0.909	1442	0.574
LuckyAgent2022	<u>0.301</u>	<u>0.250</u>	<u>0.221</u>	<u>0.551</u>	1310	<u>0.338</u>

In the collusion track, we only had two agents (CharliesAgent and M5) so a single round was conducted. The M5 agent from Tokyo University of Agriculture and Technology, Japan was able to achieve 0.7% extra profit due to its collusion strategy (i.e., over what it could achieve when collusion was turned off), winning it an honourable mention.

Taken together, these results suggest that the strategies submitted to SCML 2022 were an improvement over the ones submitted to SCML2021 in all tracks. The more straightforward challenge of the OneShot track was almost met, with a maximum profit of around 12% of a theoretical expectation of no more than 15%, with still some room for improvement. The Standard and Collusion challenges are still proving too hard, with hardly any profit being made even by top agents. This highlights the difficulty in translating advances in automated negotiation research to the complexity of the real world.

Table 3. Results for the SCML OneShot track ordered by the score in the finals. Agents with statistically insignificant score differences according to the factorial t-test are given the same rank. The finals round shows two scores for the two runs with and without SCML2021's winners.

Agent	Qualifications			Finals					
	Rank	Instances	Score	Rank		Instances		Score	
				First	Second	First	Second	First	Second
PatientAgent	1	1200	11,209	1	1	5,000	3,500	11,430	10,991
NewGentle	2	1200	10,320	2	2	5,000	3,500	10,625	10,463
AgentSAS	2	1200	10,400	3	3	5,000	3,500	10,593	10,399
AgentNeko	2	1200	10,611	4	4	5,000	3,500	10,403	10,115
EVEAgent	7	1200	9,902	5	4	5,000	3,500	10,328	9,968
LearningAdaptive	2	1200	10,381	6	6	5,000	3,500	10,131	9,608
AgentRM	2	1200	10,215	7	7	5,000	3,500	9,705	9,302
AdamAgent	8	1200	9,658	7	8	5,000	3,500	9,620	8,555
Agent112*	9	1200	9,473	9		5,000	3,500	8740	
Agent74*	10	1200	9,353	10		5,000	3,500	8317	
AdaptivePercentile	11	1200	9,036						
UCOneshot	12	1200	8,273						
AdaptiveQIAgent	12	1200	8,092						
MMMPersonalized	14	1200	7,517						
Agent125	14	1200	7,347						

Table 4. Results for the SCML Standard track ordered by the score in the finals. Agents with statistically insignificant score differences according to the factorial t-test are given the same rank.

Agent	Qualifications			Finals		
	Rank	Instances	Score	Rank	Instances	Score
Lobster	1	5,000	72	1	1,000	−96
M5	2	5,000	−264	2	1,000	−155
ArtisanKangaroo*	4	5,000	−386	3	1,000	−186
CharliesAgent	3	5,000	−354	4	1,000	−358
SkyAgent	5	5,000	−851	5	1,000	−1,041
SmartAgent	6	5,000	−991			
SalesAgent	6	5,000	−1,080			

5   Conclusion and Discussion

This chapter describes the 13th annual ANAC, held in 2022 and reports the results of the completion. The competition comprised two leagues where ANL focused on incorporating learning from past negotiations and SCML focused on strategic decision-making on whom to negotiate with and how to negotiate to maximize the overall profit in a supply chain environment.

The chapter makes the complete setup of ANAC 2022 available to the broader negotiation research community. We hope that the addressed challenges in both leagues will drag the attention of more participants and they can get benefit from insights given by the winning agents. We plan to organize the next competition in conjunction with AAMAS 2023, in London.

Acknowledgments. ANAC2022 was supported by sponsors (NEC-AIST AI Cooperative Research Laboratory, BIRD INITIATIVE, TU Delft, and CWI). This research was (partly) funded by the Vidi project COMBINE (VI.Vidi.203.044) and the Hybrid Intelligence Center(024.004.022), programmes funded through the Netherlands Organisation for Scientific Research, and by EU H2020 projects "Humane AI Net" under contract # 952026 and TAILOR under GA No 952215.

References

1. Aydoğan, R., Festen, D., Hindriks, K.V., Jonker, C.M.: Alternating offers protocols for multilateral negotiation. In: Fujita, K., et al. (eds.) Modern Approaches to Agent-based Complex Automated Negotiation. SCI, vol. 674, pp. 153–167. Springer, Cham (2017). https://doi.org/10.1007/978-3-319-51563-2_10
2. Aydoğan, R., Fujita, K., Baarslag, T., Jonker, C.M., Ito, T.: ANAC 2018: repeated multilateral negotiation league. In: The 33rd Annual Conference of the Japanese Society for Artificial Intelligence, Japan (2019)
3. Baarslag, T., Aydoğan, R., Hindriks, K.V., Fuijika, K., Ito, T., Jonker, C.M.: The automated negotiating agents competition, 2010–2015. AI Mag. **36**(4), 115–118 (2015). http://www.aaai.org/ojs/index.php/aimagazine/article/view/2609
4. Baarslag, T., et al.: Evaluating practical negotiating agents: results and analysis of the 2011 international competition. Artif. Intell. **198**, 73–103 (2013). https://doi.org/10.1016/j.artint.2012.09.004
5. Baarslag, T., Hindriks, K., Jonker, C.M., Kraus, S., Lin, R.: The first automated negotiating agents competition (ANAC 2010). In: Ito, T., Zhang, M., Robu, V., Fatima, S., Matsuo, T. (eds.) New Trends in Agent-based Complex Automated Negotiations, Series of Studies in Computational Intelligence, pp. 113–135. Springer, Heidelberg (2012). https://doi.org/10.1007/978-3-642-24696-8_7
6. Fujita, K., Aydoğan, R., Baarslag, T., Hindriks, K., Ito, T., Jonker, C.: The sixth automated negotiating agents competition (ANAC 2015). In: Fujita, K., et al. (eds.) Modern Approaches to Agent-based Complex Automated Negotiation. SCI, vol. 674, pp. 139–151. Springer, Cham (2017). https://doi.org/10.1007/978-3-319-51563-2_9
7. Fujita, K., Aydoğan, R., Baarslag, T., Ito, T., Jonker, C.: The fifth automated negotiating agents competition (ANAC 2014). In: Fukuta, N., Ito, T., Zhang, M., Fujita, K., Robu, V. (eds.) Recent Advances in Agent-based Complex Automated

Negotiation. SCI, vol. 638, pp. 211–224. Springer, Cham (2016). https://doi.org/10.1007/978-3-319-30307-9_13

8. Jonker, C.M., Aydoğan, R., Baarslag, T., Fujita, K., Ito, T., Hindriks, K.: Automated negotiating agents competition (ANAC). In: Proceedings of the Thirty-First AAAI Conference on Artificial Intelligence (AAAI-2017), pp. 5070–5072. AAAI Press (2017)

9. Mohammad, Y., Viqueira, E.A., Ayerza, N.A., Greenwald, A., Nakadai, S., Morinaga, S.: Supply chain management world. In: Baldoni, M., Dastani, M., Liao, B., Sakurai, Y., Zalila Wenkstern, R. (eds.) PRIMA 2019. LNCS (LNAI), vol. 11873, pp. 153–169. Springer, Cham (2019). https://doi.org/10.1007/978-3-030-33792-6_10

10. Nowak, M.A.: Five rules for the evolution of cooperation. Science 314(5805), 1560–1563 (2006). https://doi.org/10.1126/science.1133755

11. Rubinstein, A.: Perfect equilibrium in a bargaining model. Econometrica 50(1), 97–109 (1982). http://www.jstor.org/stable/1912531

12. Williams, C.R., Robu, V., Gerding, E.H., Jennings, N.R.: An overview of the results and insights from the third automated negotiating agents competition (ANAC2012). In: Marsa-Maestre, I., Lopez-Carmona, M.A., Ito, T., Zhang, M., Bai, Q., Fujita, K. (eds.) Novel Insights in Agent-based Complex Automated Negotiation. SCI, vol. 535, pp. 151–162. Springer, Tokyo (2014). https://doi.org/10.1007/978-4-431-54758-7_9

13. (Ya'akov) Gal, K., Ilany, L.: The fourth automated negotiation competition. In: Fujita, K., Ito, T., Zhang, M., Robu, V. (eds.) Next Frontier in Agent-based Complex Automated Negotiation. SCI, vol. 596, pp. 129–136. Springer, Tokyo (2015). https://doi.org/10.1007/978-4-431-55525-4_8

AhBuNe Agent: Winner of the Eleventh International Automated Negotiating Agent Competition (ANAC 2020)

Ahmet Burak Yildirim[1]([✉])[iD], Nezih Sunman[1,3][iD], and Reyhan Aydoğan[1,2][iD]

[1] Computer Science, Özyeğin University, Istanbul, Turkey
{burak.yildirim,nezih.sunman}@ozu.edu.tr, reyhan.aydogan@ozyegin.edu.tr
[2] Delft University of Technology, Interactive Intelligence Group, Delft,
The Netherlands
[3] Corporate Technology, Siemens A.S., Istanbul, Turkey

Abstract. The International Automated Negotiating Agent Competition introduces a new challenge each year to facilitate the research on agent-based negotiation and provide a test benchmark. ANAC 2020 addressed the problem of designing effective agents that do not know their users' complete preferences in addition to their opponent's negotiation strategy. Accordingly, this paper presents the negotiation strategy of the winner agent called "AhBuNe Agent". The proposed heuristic-based bidding strategy checks whether it has sufficient orderings to reason about its complete preferences and accordingly decides whether to sacrifice some utility in return for preference elicitation. While making an offer, it uses the most-desired known outcome as a reference and modifies the content of the bid by adopting a concession-based strategy. By analyzing the content of the given ordered bids, the importance ranking of the issues is estimated. As our agent adopts a fixed time-based concession strategy and takes the estimated issue importance ranks into account, it determines to what extent the issues are to be modified. The evaluation results of the ANAC 2020 show that our agent beats the other participating agents in terms of the received individual score.

Keywords: Automated negotiation · Agent competition · Partial preference ordering · Negotiation strategy

1 Introduction

Up to this point, various research challenges have been addressed in agent-based negotiation, where intelligent autonomous agents negotiate with each other or their human counterpart on behalf of their users [9,10,17,22]. The main challenges can be listed as generating bids under uncertainty about their opponent [7,14], learning the opponent's preferences and strategies during the negotiation [6,25], and determining when to accept the opponent's offer [8,21]. Researchers aim to design effective negotiation strategies to beat opponents and maximize their received utility.

In this well-established research field, various negotiation strategies have been proposed so far. With the intention of providing a public benchmark to rigorously evaluate and compare those strategies, an international competition called Automated Negotiating Agent Competition (ANAC) has been organized since 2010 [13]. Initially, the competition focused on bilateral multi-issue closed negotiation where the agents have linear additive utility functions and negotiate with their opponents under a time-based deadline. Over the years, organizers have introduced various research topics such as reasoning non-linear utility functions in large-scaled negotiation domains [5,18], multilateral negotiations (i.e., having more than one opponent) [11], repeated negotiations [2], human-agent negotiations [19], diplomacy game challenges [12] and supply chain management [20].

Since it may not be trivial to elicit the user's complete preferences in terms of a linear utility function, the challenge of designing a negotiating agent having only its user's partial qualitative preference information came out in ANAC 2019 [4]. The following year, the organizers extended this challenge by introducing a variant of the Stacked Alternating Offers Protocol (SAOP) in which agents are not only able to generate offers or accept their opponent's counter-offers but also ask some preference elicitation questions to their users to reduce the uncertainty about their preferences.

There are a few studies regarding the design of effective agents with partial preferences in the literature. Aydoğan and Yolum present some heuristic approaches for partial preferences represented in terms of Conditional Preference Networks (CP-Nets) by exploiting the structure of the induced preferences graphs [3]. Furthermore, Tsimpoukis et al. propose to use a linear programming approach to estimate the agent's utility function given a set of pairwise comparisons of outcomes [24]. This work is mainly based on the approach to estimating the weights for multiple attributes in a composite criterion using pairwise comparisons [23].

We propose a heuristic-based negotiation strategy that can work under the desired protocol allowing agents to ask preference elicitation questions as well as make offers. Given the partial information about preferences, it first checks whether it has sufficient orderings to make reasoning about its complete preferences. Accordingly, it decides whether to sacrifice some utility in return for preference elicitation. In the case of making an offer, it uses the best-desired known outcome as a reference and modifies the content of the bid by adopting a concession-based strategy. Our agent analyzes the content of the given ordered bids to estimate the importance ranking of the issues. By adopting a fixed time-based concession strategy and taking the estimated issue importance ranks into account, it determines to what extent the issues are to be modified. The evaluation results of ANAC 2020 show that our agent beats the other participating agents in terms of the received individual score.

The rest of this paper is organized as follows: Sect. 2 provides the necessary background for ANAC 2020 negotiation setting while Sect. 3 explains the proposed heuristic-based negotiation strategy. Section 4 describes the experimental setup and reports the achieved results in the competition. Finally, Sect. 5 concludes the paper and discusses ideas and plans for future work.

2   ANAC 2020 Negotiation Setting

In ANAC 2020, GeniusWeb [16] framework is used to run the negotiation simulations in which agents negotiate with each other by following the Stacked Human Alternating Offers Protocol (SHAOP), which is an extension of SAOP [1]. In line with the underlying research challenge, a partial preference profile is given to each agent instead of their utility functions directly. That is, agents can compare some pair of outcomes according to the given profile under the given partial information about their own user preferences. However, the system has complete utility functions for its users and allows agents to query unknown preference orderings of some outcomes with a cost of a certain utility. As Fig. 1 summarizes the interaction among negotiating agents according to the SHAOP, one of the agents initiates the negotiation with an offer, and the negotiation is held in a turn-taking fashion. In each round, an agent can perform one of the following actions:

1. Requesting elicitation
2. Accepting the offer
3. Making a counteroffer (i.e., rejecting and overriding the previous offer)
4. Walking away (i.e., ending the negotiation without any agreement)

An oracle user represents an abstract agent having access to its user's complete preferences in terms of a linear additive utility function. It can compare the bids according to the given utility function and respond to the agent's preference queries. In other words, the oracle informs its agent by providing the order of the bids without exposing their utility values so that it expands the knowledge of its agent.

This process continues until an agreement or a deadline (e.g. 100 rounds) is reached. If the agents cannot reach an agreement by the given deadline, the negotiation fails. In such a case, both negotiating parties receive the utility of their reservation bid given by the GeniusWeb framework. Note that the agents know their own reservation bid. As seen in Fig. 1, agents can elicit more information about their user's preferences but each elicitation request penalizes the score of the agents with an elicitation cost. In elicitation queries, agents aim to learn the bids in a given list that are less preferred over a certain bid. For example, if there are five bids in the list and a particular bid μ, the system will return which bids out of those five bids are less preferred over μ according to

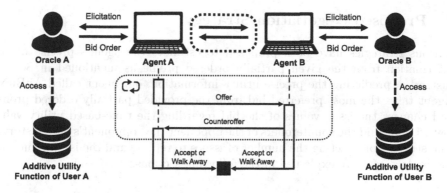

Fig. 1. Negotiation setting of ANAC 2020.

the complete preferences. At the end of the negotiation, the scores of the agents are calculated as the user utilities of the final agreement lowered with their total penalty. Winners are determined based on the average of the scores they earned in the tournament.

In this setting, a negotiation scenario consists of $I = \{1, 2, \ldots, n\}$ negotiation issues (or attributes) whose domain values are represented by $\mathcal{D} = \{D_1, \ldots, D_n\}$. An outcome is represented by o, while Ω represents the set of all possible outcomes in the negotiation domain (i.e., $D_1 \times D_2 \times \ldots \times D_n$). The agents' preferences are represented by means of linear additive utility functions in the form of:

$$\mathcal{U}(o) = \sum_{k \in I} w_k \times V_k(o[k]) \tag{1}$$

where w_k represents the importance of the negotiation issue k for the agent, $o[k]$ represents the value for issue k in outcomes o, and $V_k(.)$ is the valuation function for issue k, which returns the desirability of the issue value. Without losing generality, it is assumed that $\sum_{k \in I} w_k = 1$ and the domain of $V_k(.)$ is in the range of $[0, 1]$ for any k.

The total ordered profile is a set of outcome pairs $\mathcal{P}$ such that $\forall_{i \neq j} o_i, o_j \in \Omega$ $\wedge\ o_i \succ o_j, (o_i, o_j) \in \mathcal{P}$ where $o_i \succ o_j$ denotes that the outcome o_i is strictly preferred over o_j. In such a profile, every outcome pair is comparable. $\mathcal{P}' \subset \mathcal{P}$ denotes the partial ordered profile. The set of unique bids, outcomes, inside a total ordered profile $\mathcal{P}$ and a partially ordered profile $\mathcal{P}'$ are represented by B and B', respectively.

In the following sections, the partially ordered profiles of the agent and the opponent are denoted by B'_A and B'_O, respectively. Also, the most preferred bid in a partially ordered profile B' is represented by B'^*.

3 Proposed Negotiation Strategy

Various strategies have been proposed to estimate the agent's precise utility information from the given partially ordered profile as mentioned in Sect. 1. Instead of predicting the precise utility information, our agent called AhBuNe Agent takes the most preferred bid from the provided partially ordered profile and changes the issue values of the bid regarding the time-based utility value lower bound and the counteroffers of the opponent (i.e., opponent's offer history). The strategy of selecting the number of issues to replace and the issue values for the replacement are explained in the following sections.

3.1 Preference Elicitation

Agents are allowed to know only the preference order $\mathcal{P}'$ of a proper subset B' of all possible bids B. Here, the main challenge is to design a strategy for preference elicitation, which allows the agents to acquire the unknown preference order of a given bid among partially ordered bids. Using an elicitation strategy, the agents sacrifice some utility (i.e., elicitation cost e_c) to perceive their preferences better. AhBuNe Agent utilizes an elicitation strategy applied in two different phases of the negotiation session. In this strategy, our agent calculates the maximum number of elicitation n_e to prevent being penalized significantly by their costs, see Eq. 2. For this purpose, the maximum elicitation penalization is determined as 0.05. By dividing this constant value by the elicitation cost defined in the competition setting e_c, the allowed maximum number of elicitation n_e is found. Note that all constant values used in our strategy are determined empirically.

$$n_e = \frac{0.05}{e_c} \qquad (2)$$

Before the Negotiation Session Begins. Before starting the negotiation, AhBuNe Agent elicits n_b random bids to increase the number of ordered bids in B'_A so as to converge to the total ordering of all bids with respect to the agent's preferences. n_b is determined by the function given in Eq. 3, where $|\Omega|$ denotes the number of all possible bids in the given negotiation scenario.

$$n_b = \begin{cases} \max(\min(|\Omega| * 0.1 - |B'_A|, n_e), 0) & |\Omega| \leq 100 \\ \max(\min(10 - |B'_A|, n_e), 0) & otherwise \end{cases} \qquad (3)$$

For the domains containing less than 100 bids, we observed that the agent should know the order of at least 10% of all possible bids. If there are more than 100 bids in the domain, the minimum number of bids to be known is set to 10. If the agent initially knows only the order of less than the minimum number of bids determined above, it elicits preferences of the randomly selected n_b bids. Note that it does not exceed the number of allowed elicitation n_e. Accordingly, the agent updates B'_A after performing n_b elicitation and uses the updated partially ordered profile in the offering strategy.

In the Last Rounds. In the last rounds of the negotiation, where time t is over 0.98, our agent aims to find the most preferred bid among the opponent's previous offers. To find the target bid, the agent keeps the history of the bids offered by the opponent during the negotiation session B_{O_H}. In the last rounds, it calculates the number of conceded issue values of each bid offered by the opponent $B^i_{O_H} \in B_{O_H}$. The number of conceded issue values is calculated as the Levenshtein distance [15] L^i, between $B^i_{O_H}$ and the first offered bid by the opponent, which is assumed to be the opponent's most preferred bid B'^*_O as shown in Eq. 4 and Eq. 5 where D denotes Hamming distance.

$$D(a,b) = \begin{cases} 1 & a \neq b \\ 0 & otherwise \end{cases} \tag{4}$$

$$L^i = \sum_{k \in I} D(B'^*_O[k], B^i_{O_H}[k]) \tag{5}$$

Our agent finds the opponent's most conceded bids by sorting them according to their L^i distances. By taking n_e into account, it asks for the preference ordering of those opponent's most conceded bids one by one in descending order. Consequently, it learns the order of those bids according to its own preferences. Iterating from the most preferred one to the least, if the selected bid is acceptable for the agent (see Sect. 3.5), the agent offers that bid towards the end of the negotiation.

As a result, our agent offers an acceptable bid from the opponent's offer history, which means that the bid was acceptable for the opponent in a part of the negotiation session, in order to reach an agreement. If none of these bids are acceptable, the agent follows its default offering strategy explained in Sect. 3.4.

3.2 Estimating the Importance Order of the Issues

AhBuNe Agent extracts information from the partially ordered profile by focusing on the importance order of the issues to be able to decide whether a given bid is acceptable or not. In the given partial ordering, the ordered bids are considered as a list with indexes starting from 0 to $|B'_A|$. The importance of the bids is represented by their indexes in the list. For instance, assume that our agent has the partial ordering of the bids shown in Table 1. In the given example, the first row of the table indicates the least preferred bid.

Table 1. An example partial ordering list of an agent. Each column represents an issue and each row represents a bid.

Index	Music	Invitation	Drinks	Cleanup	Food	Location
0	DJ	Custom, Handmade	Catering	Special Equipment	Chips and Nuts	Ballroom
1	Band	Custom, Handmade	Non-Alcoholic	Special Equipment	Finger-Food	Ballroom
2	MP3	Photo	Catering	Hired Help	Finger-Food	Your Dorm
3	Band	Photo	Catering	Hired Help	Catering	Your Dorm
4	MP3	Photo	Non-Alcoholic	Hired Help	Catering	Party Tent
5	MP3	Custom, Handmade	Non-Alcoholic	Specialized Materials	Catering	Your Dorm
6	DJ	Custom, Handmade	Handmade Cocktails	Special Equipment	Catering	Ballroom
7	Band	Plain	Beer Only	Special Equipment	Handmade Food	Your Dorm
8	Band	Plain	Non-Alcoholic	Special Equipment	Finger-Food	Party Tent
9	MP3	Plain	Non-Alcoholic	Special Equipment	Catering	Party Tent
10	MP3	Custom, Printed	Beer Only	Special Equipment	Chips and Nuts	Party Room
11	Band	Photo	Catering	Water And Soup	Finger-Food	Party Room
12	MP3	Custom, Printed	Beer Only	Specialized Materials	Chips and Nuts	Party Room
13	Band	Custom, Printed	Handmade Cocktails	Special Equipment	Chips and Nuts	Party Tent
14	DJ	Custom, Printed	Beer Only	Water And Soup	Finger-Food	Party Tent
15	DJ	Custom, Printed	Handmade Cocktails	Hired Help	Handmade Food	Party Tent
16	DJ	Custom, Printed	Non-Alcoholic	Water And Soup	Finger-Food	Party Tent
17	MP3	Custom, Printed	Handmade Cocktails	Special Equipment	Handmade Food	Party Tent
18	Band	Custom, Printed	Beer Only	Water And Soup	Handmade Food	Party Tent
19	MP3	Custom, Printed	Handmade Cocktails	Water And Soup	Catering	Party Room

As explained in Sect. 3.1, the elicited bids, if they exist, are also incorporated into this list according to their learned preference order and the indices are updated accordingly. Our agent aims to estimate the importance order of each issue $k \in I$ by making inferences from the indexes. Consequently, it groups the indices of the bids by issue values for each issue. While finding the importance score of an issue, the mean index value of each issue value and their standard deviation is calculated as in Table 2.

Table 2. Example importance calculation of the music issue. The standard deviation of the mean index value of each issue value corresponds to the importance of the issue.

Issue values			
DJ	Band	MP3	
0	1	2	
6	3	4	
14	7	5	
15	8	9	
16	11	10	
-	13	12	
-	18	17	
-	-	19	**Standard deviation**
10.2	8.714	9.75	0.7618

For simplicity, our intuition is that if the standard deviation of the average indices for possible issue values is higher, it is considered a more important issue for the user. Here, the primary assumption is that all issue values are equally distributed in the given partial ordering of the bids. Without a doubt, it may not hold in all cases. It depends on the distribution of the values in the given partially ordered bids. By following the example above, the estimated importance order of the issues is listed in Table 3.

Table 3. Estimated importance order of the issues according to the standard deviations of the average indexes of their issue values.

Importance order	Issue	Standard deviation
1	Location	5.5658
2	Invitation	5.2009
3	Drinks	4.5874
4	Cleanup	4.2054
5	Food	2.9853
6	Music	0.7618

3.3   Opponent Modeling

When we analyze the strategies used by the state-of-the-art negotiating agents, we can see that they mostly offer their most preferred bid in the first round not to leave money on the table. Based on this observation, we use a heuristic in our opponent modeling, which assumes that the opponent's first offer is his/her most preferred bid. This bid is used to estimate the lower boundary of the opponent's target utility u_o^*. It is estimated by using the Levenshtein distance with an additional penalization value, which is explained in the following sections.

Estimating Opponent's Partial Ordering. As the opponent's partially ordered profile B'_O is not known by our agent, we adopt the same indexing approach explained in Sect. 3.2 to estimate it. Note that B'^i_O represents the bid at index i. Our agent keeps the history of its opponent's previous offers in a list similar to our partial ordering structure to estimate the opponent's preference list. Here, we assume that the first offer made by the opponent is the most preferred outcome, and it concedes over time. The opponent may not constantly concede during the negotiation and offer the same bid in different time slots. In such a case, we consider the time slot of its first appearance in the bid history. Using the estimated partial order, our agent can determine whether or not its opponent concedes enough.

Estimating the Most Preferred Issue Values. The opponent's most preferred issue values are determined by considering its bid history. It is assumed that the opponent offers his/her most preferred bids in the first rounds; therefore, the issue values that appeared in those rounds are considered the most preferred issue values. The target concession ratio of the opponent $1 - u_o^*$ is calculated by taking the difference between the maximum utility value that can be obtained (i.e., one) and the target utility value of the opponent u_o^*. Considering the target concession ratio of the opponent, we calculate the value of n_{mp} as in Eq. 6, which denotes the number of the most preferred bids consisting of the most preferred issue values. The set of most preferred issue values K_{mp}, see Eq. 7, is found by taking the unique issue values occurring in the most preferred n_{mp} bids.

$$n_{mp} = floor(|B_O'| * (1 - u_o^*)) \tag{6}$$

$$K_{mp} = \{B_O'^i[k] \mid k \in I, i \in [|B_O'| - n_{mp} - 1, |B_O'| - 1]\} \tag{7}$$

Estimating to What Extent the Opponent Concedes. To decide whether a given bid satisfies the opponent's target utility, it is assumed that each issue has a similar effect on the utility value, which is $1/|I|$. Equation 8 denotes to what extent the opponent concedes. If the issue values v in the given bids appear in the most preferred bid, then there is no concession (i.e., zero). If it does not exist in K_{mp}, that corresponds to a big concession. Otherwise, it corresponds to a small concession.

$$C(v) = \begin{cases} 0 & v \in B_O'^* \\ 2 & v \notin K_{mp} \wedge v \notin B_O'^* \\ 1 & otherwise \end{cases} \tag{8}$$

We estimate the approximate utility value $\hat{u}$ of a given bid o for the opponent as shown in Eq. 9.

$$\hat{u}(o) = \frac{(|I| - 1) - \sum_{k \in I} C(o[k])}{|I|} \tag{9}$$

Our agent desires that the opponent concedes at least as we do. Therefore, it generates an offer whose estimated utility for the opponent is less than our estimated utility lower bound.

3.4   Offering Strategy

Our agent follows a basic offering strategy changing the issue values of the most preferred bid considering a time-based lower boundary for the target utility. We randomly generate a bid meeting the lower utility boundary condition. In the following part, we explain how we calculate this boundary.

Lower Target Utility Boundary Curve. We adopt a time-based concession strategy where we calculate the lower target utility (TU) boundary. It represents the minimum target utility $TU_{min}(t)$ that the agent can concede to at a specific time t during the negotiation. The lower utility boundary calculation is given in Eq. 10. In the equation, t and $p_e(t)$ represent the time between $[0,1]$ and the total elicitation penalization at time t, respectively. $p_e(t)$ is used to take the penalization cost into account when concerning the lower boundary of TU. The plotted version of the curve is shown in Fig. 2, in which the penalized elicitation cost variable is neglected because it is a dynamic variable that can vary during the negotiation.

$$TU_{min}(t) = \begin{cases} -(t - 0.25)^2 + 0.9 + p_e(t) & 0 \le t < 0.5 \\ -(1.5*(t - 0.7))^2 + 0.9 + p_e(t) & 0.5 \le t < 0.7 \\ 3.25*t^2 - 6.155*t + 3.6105 + p_e(t) & otherwise \end{cases} \quad (10)$$

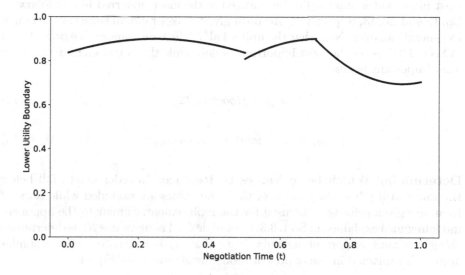

Fig. 2. Lower target utility boundary curve.

First, our agent is reluctant to reveal its most preferred offer. Therefore, instead of starting with the most preferred offer, as usual, our agent initially makes a random offers whose estimated utility is above ~ 0.8 and slightly increases this boundary to 0.9 by hoping that its moves can be considered as a concession by the opponent (i.e., misleading the opponent about its own preferences). Then, it slightly decreases the lower boundary in order to make the opponent think that our agent is insisting on its most preferred bids because we sent similar bids at the beginning of the session.

By adopting a sarcastic movement again, the agent increases its lower boundary to make the opponent think that it is decreasing its target utility value the second time. We hope that the opponent perceives it as a concession and accepts one of our offers made in this phase. While approaching the deadline, our agent starts conceding to reach an agreement.

In the last moments (i.e., after reaching 98% of the negotiation deadline), instead of randomly generating bids, our agent elicits a subset of the opponent's bid history as explained in Sect. 3.1 to offer the most suitable one with the aim of increasing the chance of agreement.

Determining the Number of Issues to Be Replaced. While making an offer, our agent calculates the maximum number of issues to be changed, n_{ch}, based on the lower boundary of TU as seen in Eq. 11.

$$n_{ch}(t) = floor(TU_{min}(t) * |I|) \tag{11}$$

Then, it estimates the number of the most important issues (n_{mi}) and the least important issues (n_{li}) to be changed in the most preferred bid by following Eq. 12 and Eq. 13, respectively. Accordingly, it makes random issue value changes to generate an offer. Note that the upper half of the issue importance order found in Sect. 3.2 denotes the most important issues, while the bottom half denotes the least important issues.

$$n_{mi} = floor(n_{ch}/2) \tag{12}$$

$$n_{li} = n_{ch} \mod 2 + floor(n_{ch}/2) \tag{13}$$

Determining Which Issue Values to Replace. In order not to fall below the lower utility boundary, some of the issue values are excluded while some of them are given priority to be used for the replacement. Similar to the opponent modeling idea explained in Sect. 3.3, a set of desired issue values K_d is determined using the most important n_d bids. Note that n_d is calculated with a similar approach explained in the opponent modeling strategy, see Eq. 14.

$$n_d(t) = floor(|B'_A| * (1 - TU_{min}(t))) + 1 \tag{14}$$

Similar to the desired issue value set, the set of undesired issue values K_u is formed by considering the least important n_u bids. The issue values inside K_d are ignored in this process. The intuition behind this idea is that the issue values in the most preferred bids are more likely to be the most desired ones even if they exist in the least preferred bids. It is worth noting that n_u is determined by the distance between the current utility lower bound $TU_{min}(t)$ and the lowest value of the utility lower bound curve (i.e., $TU_{min}(1)$) as shown in Eq. 15.

$$n_u(t) = floor(|B'_A| * (TU_{min}(t) - TU_{min}(1))) + 1 \tag{15}$$

When determining a value of an issue for replacement, the values in K_u are not allowed to be used if there exists an alternative issue value. On the other hand, if the selected value is in K_d, then n_{mi} or n_{li} are decreased by one concerning the importance of the issue changed. Otherwise, both n_{mi} and n_{li} are decreased by one regardless of whether the issue is less or more important not to fall below the lower utility boundary.

Furthermore, the most crucial part of the issue value selection process is that the changed issue values are desired to be taken, if possible, from the values of the opponent's most preferred bid so that the generated bid becomes more acceptable for the opponent. After replacing the issue values, if the randomly generated bid satisfies all the conditions explained above and our lower boundary of target utility is higher than the opponent's one, then the generated bid is sent as an offer. Otherwise, we generate different randomly generated bids repeatedly until one of them satisfies the conditions.

3.5   Acceptance Strategy

If the opponent's offer has an estimated utility value greater than 0.9, AhBuNe Agent accepts this offer regardless of the lower utility boundary of the opponent. If this condition is not satisfied, AhBuNe Agent uses the strategy explained in Sect. 3.4 to estimate the lower utility boundary of a given bid. Then, using the opponent modeling strategy explained in Sect. 3.3, it also estimates the utility value of the bid for the opponent as well. As the last step, it compares these utility values. If the lower boundary of our utility value is greater than the utility of the opponent, and the utility lower bound $TU_{min}(t)$ at time t is satisfied, it accepts the offer. Otherwise, it makes a counteroffer using the algorithm explained in Sect. 3.4.

4   Evaluation

In ANAC 2020, 13 agents are submitted by eight institutions from seven countries. Scores of the agents are calculated by subtracting the average penalty values from the average received utility values of the tournament results. The finalists, the best-performing five agents, and the winner are determined with respect to their calculated scores. The tournament setup and the overall results are reported below.

4.1   Setup of the Tournament

The submitted agents are evaluated by organizing a tournament on the GeniusWeb 1.4.4 platform. The deadline in terms of rounds is set to 100 rounds. Four different negotiation domains were used in the competition where two partial preference profiles exist per domain. In the tournament, each negotiation session is run 10 times which results in 1560 negotiations per scenario. Each negotiation scenario is run with two different elicitation costs 0.01 and 0.001. The details of the negotiation scenarios used in the competition are explained in Table 4.

Table 4. Negotiation scenarios used in the ANAC 2020 tournament.

Domain name	Domain size	# Issues	# Partial bids	Reservation value
Flight Booking	$4 \times 3 \times 3 = 36$	3	10	~ 0.6
Japan Trip	$4 \times 4 \times 4 \times 3 = 192$	4	50	~ 0.2
Fitness	$5 \times 4 \times 4 \times 4 \times 4 = 1280$	5	50	~ 0.2
Party	$4 \times 4 \times 4 \times 4 \times 3 \times 4 = 3072$	6	75	~ 0.6

4.2 Results

In order to analyze the tournament results elaborately, we used ANAC 2020 tournament logs to compare the characteristics of the agents in terms of three metrics as follows:

- **Acceptance Ratio:** It is calculated by dividing the number of agreements by the number of total negotiation sessions.
- **Average Social Welfare:** It corresponds to the average of the social welfare of all agreements. Note that social welfare is the sum of the utilities of the negotiation outcome for both parties.
- **Average Individual Acceptance Utility:** It is the average of the utilities received by each agent and their opponents.

The tournament results of the finalist agents are provided in Table 5. It can be observed that AhBuNe Agent and AgentKT outperformed other agents in terms of average social welfare and average acceptance utility even though their acceptance ratios are lower than the Hamming Agent and the Shine Agent.

Table 5. ANAC 2020 tournament results.

Agent name	Acceptance ratio	Average social welfare	Average acceptance utility	
			Agent	Opponent
AhBuNe agent	0.5249	**1.4781**	**0.8611**	**0.6169**
Hamming agent	**0.6966**	1.4369	0.7510	0.6858
Shine agent	**0.6751**	1.4540	0.7428	0.7112
AgentKT	0.5354	**1.4740**	**0.8649**	**0.6091**
ANGELparty	0.4217	1.4579	0.8237	0.6342

For a better understanding of the tournament results, the performances of the finalist agents are analyzed in each domain as shown in Fig. 3. In all negotiation scenarios, our agent took either first or second place. Besides, there is a significant performance difference between our agent and Hamming Agent in the Flight Booking domain, which is the smallest domain in the tournament.

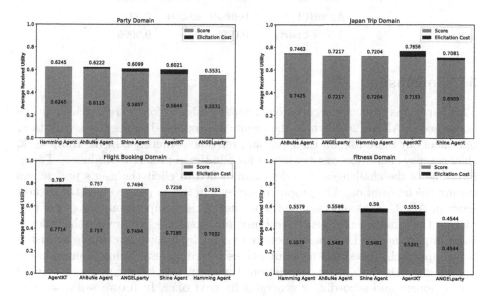

Fig. 3. ANAC 2020 tournament results per each domain.

Table 6 shows the overall results of the tournament per finalist agents in terms of received average utility, penalty, and score, respectively. As is seen, effective usage of preference elicitation plays a crucial role in the agents' success in terms of their final scores. The average utilities received by AhBuNe Agent and AgentKT are almost the same. However, AgentKT ranked in fourth place due to receiving a higher penalty score for the elicitation even though its acceptance rate is higher than ours. As a result, our agent received a higher score because of the low elicitation cost.

Furthermore, it is also seen that Hamming Agent and ANGEL Party did not perform any elicitation during their negotiation and could not outperform AhBuNe Agent. This may stem from having less information about their user's preferences. To sum up, the negotiation strategy used by AhBuNe Agent succeeded to balance the utility and the penalty scores. It is worth mentioning that there is a trade-off between preference elicitation and the cost of elicitation. As the elicitation number increases, agents get more insight into their users' preferences. However, it also causes a decrease in the received final score, which determines the winner.

Table 6. Overall ranking of ANAC 2020.

Rank	Agent name	Utility	Penalty	Score
1	AhBuNe Agent	**0.6623**	**0.0070**	**0.6554**
2	Hamming Agent	0.6484	0	0.6484
3	Shine Agent	0.6591	0.0187	0.6404
4	AgentKT	**0.6640**	0.0304	0.6336
5	ANGELparty	0.6096	0	0.6096

5   Conclusion

This paper describes our negotiation strategy designed for the research challenge addressed in ANAC 2020 where the agents are supposed to negotiate with their opponents by reasoning on their partial preference orderings. In the framework, they can pay elicitation costs in return for additional preference ordering. Therefore, one of the challenges is to determine when to elicit the user's preferences during the negotiation. The proposed strategy in this paper received the highest score in ANAC 2020 and became the winner of the competition. Instead of predicting the complete preference structure, our agent tries to predict the order of issue importance and the most preferred values by following a simple heuristic-based approach. Based on the assumptions regarding issue value changes in the opponent's bids during the negotiation, the agent infers the concession level of the opponent and accordingly generates its next offer. In future work, we plan to exploit the relationship between the structure of the utility function (i.e., additive utility function) and the given partial ordering so to get more insights into the preference ordering of the issue values and importance. It would be interesting to design an elicitation strategy not only at the beginning/end of the negotiation but also in the middle of the negotiation.

Acknowledgement. We would like to thank Prof. Dr. Catholijn Jonker, Assoc. Prof. Dr. Katsuhide Fujita, Assist. Prof. Dr. Reyhan Aydoğan, and Dr. Tim Baarslag for sharing the ANAC 2020 tournament results.

References

1. Aydoğan, R., Festen, D., Hindriks, K.V., Jonker, C.M.: Alternating offers protocols for multilateral negotiation. In: Fujita, K., et al. (eds.) Modern Approaches to Agent-based Complex Automated Negotiation. SCI, vol. 674, pp. 153–167. Springer, Cham (2017). https://doi.org/10.1007/978-3-319-51563-2_10
2. Aydogan, R., Fujita, K., Baarslag, T., Jonker, C.M., Ito, T.: ANAC 2018: repeated multilateral negotiation league. In: The 33rd Annual Conference of the Japanese Society for Artificial Intelligence, Japan (2019)
3. Aydoğan, R., Yolum, P.: Learning disjunctive preferences for negotiating effectively. In: Eighth International Joint Conference on Autonomous Agents and Multiagent Systems (AAMAS), pp. 1201–1202 (2009). https://doi.org/10.1145/1558109.1558212

4. Aydoğan, R., et al.: Challenges and main results of the automated negotiating agents competition (ANAC) 2019. In: Bassiliades, N., Chalkiadakis, G., de Jonge, D. (eds.) EUMAS/AT -2020. LNCS (LNAI), vol. 12520, pp. 366–381. Springer, Cham (2020). https://doi.org/10.1007/978-3-030-66412-1_23
5. Aydoğan, R., et al.: A baseline for non-linear bilateral negotiations: the full results of the agents competing in ANAC 2014. In: Frontiers in Artificial Intelligence: Intelligent Computational Systems, pp. 96–122. Bentham Science (2017)
6. Baarslag, T., Hendrikx, M.J.C., Hindriks, K., Jonker, C.: Learning about the opponent in automated bilateral negotiation: a comprehensive survey of opponent modeling techniques. Auton. Agent. Multi-Agent Syst. **30**, 849–898 (2015)
7. Baarslag, T., Gerding, E.H., Aydoğan, R., Schraefel, M.: Optimal negotiation decision functions in time-sensitive domains. In: 2015 IEEE/WIC/ACM International Joint Conferences on Web Intelligence (WI) and Intelligent Agent Technologies (IAT), vol. 2, pp. 190–197 (2015). https://doi.org/10.1109/WI-IAT.2015.161
8. Baarslag, T., Hindriks, K.V., Jonker, C.M.: Effective acceptance conditions in real-time automated negotiation. Decis. Support Syst. **60**, 68–77 (2014). https://doi.org/10.1016/j.dss.2013.05.021
9. Baarslag, T., Kaisers, M., Gerding, E.H., Jonker, C.M., Gratch, J.: Self-sufficient, self-directed, and interdependent negotiation systems: a roadmap toward autonomous negotiation agents. In: Karagözoğlu, E., Hyndman, K.B. (eds.) Bargaining: Current Research and Future Directions, pp. 387–406. Springer, Cham (2022). https://doi.org/10.1007/978-3-030-76666-5_18
10. Fatima, S., Kraus, S., Wooldridge, M.: Principles of Automated Negotiation. Cambridge University Press, Cambridge (2014)
11. Fujita, K., Aydoğan, R., Baarslag, T., Hindriks, K., Ito, T., Jonker, C.: The sixth automated negotiating agents competition (ANAC 2015). In: Fujita, K., et al. (eds.) Modern Approaches to Agent-based Complex Automated Negotiation. SCI, vol. 674, pp. 139–151. Springer, Cham (2017). https://doi.org/10.1007/978-3-319-51563-2_9
12. de Jonge, D., Baarslag, T., Aydoğan, R., Jonker, C., Fujita, K., Ito, T.: The challenge of negotiation in the game of diplomacy. In: Lujak, M. (ed.) AT 2018. LNCS (LNAI), vol. 11327, pp. 100–114. Springer, Cham (2019). https://doi.org/10.1007/978-3-030-17294-7_8
13. Jonker, C.M., Aydoğan, R., Baarslag, T., Fujita, K., Ito, T., Hindriks, K.: Automated negotiating agents competition (ANAC). In: Proceedings of the Thirty-First AAAI Conference on Artificial Intelligence (AAAI 2017), pp. 5070–5072. AAAI Press (2017)
14. Jonker, C.M., Aydoğan, R.: Deniz: a robust bidding strategy for negotiation support systems. In: Ito, T., Zhang, M., Aydoğan, R. (eds.) ACAN 2018. SCI, vol. 905, pp. 29–44. Springer, Singapore (2021). https://doi.org/10.1007/978-981-15-5869-6_3
15. Levenshtein, V.: Binary codes capable of correcting deletions, insertions and reversals. Soviet Phys. Doklady **10**, 707 (1966)
16. Lin, R., Kraus, S., Baarslag, T., Tykhonov, D., Hindriks, K.V., Jonker, C.M.: Genius: an integrated environment for supporting the design of generic automated negotiators. Comput. Intell. **30**(1), 48–70 (2014). https://doi.org/10.1111/j.1467-8640.2012.00463.x
17. Marsa-Maestre, I., Klein, M., Jonker, C.M., Aydoğan, R.: From problems to protocols: towards a negotiation handbook. Decis. Support Syst. 39–54 (2014)

18. Marsá-Maestre, I., López-Carmona, M.A., Klein, M., Ito, T., Fujita, K.: Addressing utility space complexity in negotiations involving highly uncorrelated, constraint-based utility spaces. Comput. Intell. **30**(1), 1–29 (2014). https://doi.org/10.1111/j.1467-8640.2012.00461.x
19. Mell, J., Gratch, J., Baarslag, T., Aydoğan, R., Jonker, C.M.: Results of the first annual human-agent league of the automated negotiating agents competition. In: In Proceedings of the 18th International Conference on Intelligent Virtual Agents, pp. 23–28. ACM (2018)
20. Mohammad, Y., Viqueira, E.A., Ayerza, N.A., Greenwald, A., Nakadai, S., Morinaga, S.: Supply chain management world. In: Baldoni, M., Dastani, M., Liao, B., Sakurai, Y., Zalila Wenkstern, R. (eds.) PRIMA 2019. LNCS (LNAI), vol. 11873, pp. 153–169. Springer, Cham (2019). https://doi.org/10.1007/978-3-030-33792-6_10
21. Razeghi, Y., Yavuz, O., Aydoğan, R.: Deep reinforcement learning for acceptance strategy in bilateral negotiations. Turk. J. Electr. Eng. Comput. Sci. **28**, 1824–1840 (2020). https://doi.org/10.3906/elk-1907-215
22. Sanchez-Anguix, V., Tunalı, O., Aydoğan, R., Julian, V.: Can social agents efficiently perform in automated negotiation? Appl. Sci. **11**(13) (2021). https://doi.org/10.3390/app11136022. https://www.mdpi.com/2076-3417/11/13/6022
23. Srinivasan, V., Shocker, A.: Estimating the weights for multiple attributes in a composite criterion using pairwise judgments. Psychometrika **38**, 473–493 (1973)
24. Tsimpoukis, D., Baarslag, T., Kaisers, M., Paterakis, N.G.: Automated negotiations under user preference uncertainty: a linear programming approach. In: Lujak, M. (ed.) AT 2018. LNCS (LNAI), vol. 11327, pp. 115–129. Springer, Cham (2019). https://doi.org/10.1007/978-3-030-17294-7_9
25. Tunalı, O., Aydoğan, R., Sanchez-Anguix, V.: Rethinking frequency opponent modeling in automated negotiation. In: An, B., Bazzan, A., Leite, J., Villata, S., van der Torre, L. (eds.) PRIMA 2017. LNCS (LNAI), vol. 10621, pp. 263–279. Springer, Cham (2017). https://doi.org/10.1007/978-3-319-69131-2_16

Agenda-Based Automated Negotiation Through Utility Decomposition

Zongcan Li(✉), Rafik Hadfi, and Takayuki Ito

Department of Social Informatics, Kyoto University, Kyoto, Japan
zongcan_li@outlook.com, {rafik.hadfi,ito}@i.kyoto-u.ac.jp

Abstract. The success of a negotiation depends mainly on the strategies of the negotiators and the problem domain. It is common for negotiators to rely on an agenda to simplify the process and reach better deals. This is particularly true when the negotiators' preferences are defined over multiple issues. Using an agenda to explore and decompose the interdependencies between the issues is one way to address this problem. This paper applies the classical divide-and-conquer approach to automated negotiations through utility decomposition and bottom-up agenda construction. The approach does not impose an agenda from the top level of the negotiations but builds it bottom-up, given the individual utility functions of the agents and the relationships between the issues. We implemented our method in a novel protocol called the Decomposable Alternating Offers Protocol (DAOP). The protocol reduces the cost of exploring the utility spaces of the agents and the generation of optimal bids. As a result, the divide-and-conquer algorithm positively influences the global performance of an automated negotiation system.

Keywords: Agent development · Automated negotiation · Multiagent systems · Preference elicitation · Automated decision-making · Human-agent interaction · Divide-and-conquer · DAOP

1 Introduction

Negotiation is a process by which several rational and self-interested parties attempt to reach an agreement [17]. The involved parties may compromise to achieve their purposes. This process of beneficial exchange happens in every aspect of people's daily lives. While negotiating with intelligent opponents such as humans, the outcome is not always guaranteed. In order to achieve a relatively optimal outcome, it is crucial to understand each other's requirements so that the negotiator can make concession appropriately.

Automated negotiation has already been addressed in different ways in research [4, 17]. The general setting involves at least two parties, where each party has preferences, strategies, and possibly an agenda [18]. A negotiation strategy is a mapping from the state of the negotiations, as understood by the negotiator, to the actions allowed by the negotiation protocol (sometimes called a mechanism) [23]. Preferences are usually represented using a function that maps the bids to their values. In the following, we

© The Author(s), under exclusive license to Springer Nature Singapore Pte Ltd. 2023
R. Hadfi et al. (Eds.): IJCAI 2022, SCI 1092, pp. 119–135, 2023.
https://doi.org/10.1007/978-981-99-0561-4_7

define an agenda as subsets of issues that the negotiators negotiate about. For instance, in the case of online trading, the agenda usually consists of the price, the quantity and the delivery methods. In the whole process, the preferences of the self-interested agents have great influence on the decision-making process.

The dynamics of the negotiations are thoroughly studied in negotiation research. An unnoticeable variation of action sequence could cause huge deviation in the expected result. The reason for this, is that often times, the issues under consideration are usually not independent when it comes to a purchase or a sale, for example, of a bundle of items on Ebay or Amazon [25]. Besides, if the agenda of the negotiation can be modeled appropriately, the value space of some issues could be so enormous that the negotiation becomes cognitively and computationally intractable [11]. To tackle the problem that most real-world negotiations face, previous research proposed to decompose contracts [9]. By evaluating the interdependence among issues in contracts, the issues could be grouped and an optimal bid selected by the mediator between two negotiators will be the final bid for both negotiators. Other methods relied on structured search and the use of agenda to simplify the contract spaces [21, 34]

This paper contributes to the negotiation research by proposing a novel negotiation strategy that uses the classical divide-and-conquer (in the rest of this paper, represented by DaC) paradigm [29]. The basic idea of the DaC paradigm is to decompose a given problem into two or more related, but simpler, sub-problems, to solve them in turn, and to compose their solutions to solve the given problem. The DaC approach is also a design pattern that can be applied to all kinds of computational problems such as optimization, prediction, and matching [10, 24, 35].

Our approach is not only applied to the elicitation phase of the negotiation, but allows the division of the complete bidding space into several sub-bids that are later negotiated individually with the opponents. The approach optimizes the global effi-ciency and intuitively simplifies a complex utility space [12]. Our proposed protocol, the Decomposable Alternating Offers Protocol (DAOP), allows the negotiators to nego-tiate over sub-bids whenever the initial bidding space is too complex to tackle. To this end, the utility functions of all negotiators are used to correctly compute the utilities of the sub-bids. This requires the decomposition of the utility functions which are difficult to handle in the presence of nonlinear relationships [6, 11, 19].

The mechanism in DAOP requires all the two parties to participate in several rounds of negotiations toward one single agreement. First, the protocol will divide an initial complete bid into sub-sets of issues. Then, the two agents negotiate over these sub-sets of issues in order to reach all sub-agreements. Finally, the DAOP will combine the sub-agreements into a complete agreement. The negotiation is finished. In addition, at any time, if the negotiation reaches the time limit, the negotiation will be terminated without any agreement. With the concept of marginal utility loss, our agents find the proper agendas in a fast and satisfactory way.

The paper is structured as follows. In the next section, we cover some of the key concepts in automated negotiation. In Sect. 3, we introduce our DaC framework. In Sect. 4, we provide the experimental results. Finally, we conclude and highlight the future directions.

2 Related Work

2.1 Automated Negotiation

The general interaction model of agent-based negotiations is shown in Fig. 1. The process starts from two humans trying to make a deal in a negotiation domain. Two artificial agents will be used to firstly elicit the preferences of the humans, and then engage in bilateral negotiation concluded with an agreement, or not.

The use of artificial agents for this task takes advantage of the rapid development of computing technologies such as Deep Learning [27] or Smart Contracts [20]. Though the agents in negotiations seem to be competing, there are benefits to cooperation through means of concession-making. This is the case when negotiations aim at win-win deals for all parties, while simultaneously reducing the time and effort, and adding significant value to system as a whole.

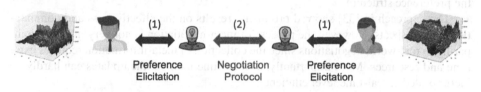

	(1)		(2)		(1)	
	Preference Elicitation		Negotiation Protocol		Preference Elicitation	

Fig. 1. In a bilateral automated negotiation, two artificial agents (1) elicit the preferences of their human counterparts, and then (2) negotiate on their behalf

The agents are essentially used to reduce the burden of eliciting complex preferences and then exchanging bids at a rate that humans cannot generally cope with [28]. The process of querying humans to learn their preferences could be costly and additional methods need to be used [5].

2.2 Utility Functions

The preferences of the negotiators are required for the agents to properly evaluate the offers of the opponents and propose offers that benefit their interests. The utility functions are therefore acquired from the negotiators' preferences. It is common practice to assume that the domains of the issues are discrete to avoid large utility spaces, which will consequently complexify the negotiations [11]. The size of the domains is only one of the obstacles on the way to put automated negotiation into real use. There are other considerations such as the shapes of utility functions. When the issues are independent, agents can aggregate the utilities of the issues by simple summation, producing linear utility functions [15]. Linear utility functions are commonly more tractable because of their regularity with respect to the value of issues.

2.3 Interdependent Issues

Interdependence between the issues is an aspect that characterizes most real-world negotiations [11]. The relationships between the issues are usually unknown between agents and even for the agent itself [28,31]. This assumption is one that we take in our proposed protocol (DAOP) in the sense that each agent starts from a "black box" of preferences, and needs to gradually extract the relationships between the issues given its own preferences. The approach here is to start by querying the utility function of the agent and based on the result, the agent could explore these relationships.

There is abundant research on interdependence extraction in negotiation [1,13]. For example, a method grouping highly interdependent issues by collecting meta-level information about the agenda in prior to the negotiation was developed and evaluated in [33]. A method was then proposed for using meta-negotiation. To better understand the influence of the input preference structure on the negotiators' performance, five parameters were defined to capture the topological and the interdependent characteristics of the preference structure.

The approach in [33] showed promising results on the effectiveness and computational cost aspects. However, the process of meta-negotiation is not very intuitive comparing to real-world negotiations since the collection of meta-information requires extra time and resources. More importantly, as an offline method, the updates can hardly be incorporated at real-time level efficiency.

2.4 Negotiation Protocols

Negotiation protocols are often defined as the rules of interaction during a negotiation. These protocols are based for example on alternating offers [3], in which negotiators take turns as they exchange possible deals. In argumentation-based protocols, agents can exchange logical sentences intended to persuade one another to change their states of mind [32]. Other protocol rely on agendas [8]. In the stacked alternating offers protocol (SAOP) all of the negotiators around the table get a turn per round; turns are shuffled randomly. One of the negotiating parties starts the negotiation with an offer that is observed by the others. Whenever an offer is made, the next party in line can take the following actions: accept the offer, reject the offer, and repeat the process. Our proposed mechanism is an adaptation of SAOP, called the decomposable alternating offers protocol (DAOP). Although all of these protocols can only influence the negotiations from the outside, they can still be regarded as mediators between the negotiators since they work between them, which also makes them an essential component of any negotiation.

2.5 Negotiation Platforms

There are a few platforms for the simulation and study of automated negotiation. The most prominent platforms are NegMAS [22] and GENIUS [14]. GENIUS is a Java-based tool that facilitates research in the area of bilateral multi-issue negotiation. It was developed comparably earlier than NegMAS, which led to abundant agent libraries [14]. GENIUS supports all kinds of bilateral negotiation mechanisms. The more recent NegMAS is a Python-based toolkit that is currently being used to study negotiations for the supply chain management (SCM) domain [23]. A supply chain is a sequence of processes by which raw materials are converted into finished goods. This process is managed by multiple independent entities (agents), whose coordination is performed according to a situated negotiation. The automated negotiating agents represent sellers and buyers located in the supply chain's upstream and downstream [23]. The GENIUS and NegMAS platforms provide little support for interdependent negotiation sessions, which are required to model situations that involve concurrent negotiations and various preference profiles. NegMAS supports more general protocols and the negotiation is not limited to the bilateral case. Moreover, the dynamical features of NegMAS allow the manipulation of all the parameters involved in the negotiation. For this reason, we choose to develop our DAOP protocol on NegMAS.

3 The Divide-and-Conquer Approach

3.1 Decomposable Alternating Offers Protocol (DAOP)

The utility space of each agent could easily become intractable with complex domains. For instance, a negotiation over 10 discrete issues with 5 possible values yields 5^{10} different possibilities for the negotiators to explore and evaluate the bids. Here, the assumption is that our DaC algorithm will make it easier for the negotiators to come up with good offers regarding the efficiency and utility gain for all the negotiations. The essence of DAOP is illustrated in Fig. 2 with a comparison to SAOP.

Essentially, the negotiators first negotiate over the subsets of issues. After reaching agreement over all subsets, the protocol will combine these sub-agreements into complete agreements. Note that the subsets of issues could overlap in the sense that they mutually affect the overall utility function.

To implement the DaC paradigm, we propose an adaptation of SAOP and call it the decomposable alternating offers protocol (DAOP). The difference between DAOP and SAOP is that, negotiations over sub-bids are permitted in DAOP. Moreover, the stacked scheme of SAOP is not required since we focus on bilateral negotiations. In SAOP, all of the negotiators around the table get a turn per round; turns are shuffled randomly. One of the negotiating parties starts the negotiation with an offer that is immediately observed by all others. Whenever an offer is made, the next party in line can take the following actions: accept the offer, reject the offer, and repeat the process [3]. The mechanism of DAOP is shown in Fig. 2 (bottom). DAOP, follows the same process with the exception that it is firstly applied to sub-offers before reaching a full agreement in the end.

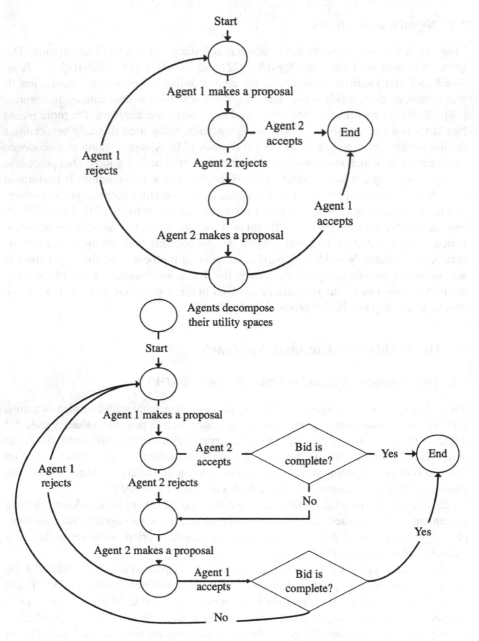

Fig. 2. Implementing the Divide-and-Conquer (DaC) approach by adapting SAOP (top) into DAOP (bottom)

3.2 Decomposition Mechanism in DAOP

When the agents attempt to negotiate over subsets of issues, the protocol will first divides the complete bidding space into m sub-bidding space Fig. 3.

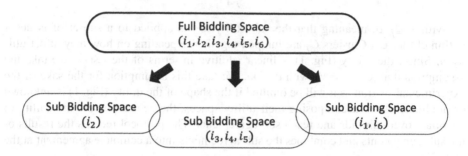

Fig. 3. Decomposition of the bidding space into 3 subspaces

As an example, when the bidding space consists of 6 issues, represented by a vector $(i_1, i_2, i_3, i_4, i_5, i_6)$, the protocol breaks the full bidding space into several sub bidding space according to the interdependency relationships among the issues. The sub bidding space can still overlap with each other because of the possible correlations between the issues. The negotiators will then evaluate each sub-space and make decisions of accepting or declining sub-offers. The functions used for evaluating the complete bid space are of course different from the ones we use for sub-bids. To infer the utility functions for evaluating sub-bids, we will decompose the original utility function.

Herein, we focus on two types of utility functions. We first assign classical linear utility functions to the agents. The utility space formed by linear utility function can be easily decomposed. In contrast, nonlinear utility functions are more complicated. The issues within a nonlinear utility are not independent, which means their utility values impact each other. Thus, the global utility depends on the relationships among the issues. Nonlinear utility functions are more often used in real-world negotiations because of the interdependency existing among the issues. However, here we take an example to explain the decomposition mechanism. Then, we will get to the more intricate settings in the next part of this paper.

The agents originally use a weighted linear utility (Fig. 1) as their preferences model to evaluate the bids.

$$u(o) = \sum_{k=1}^{n} w_k \times u_k(i_k) \tag{1}$$

where o is an offer defined as $o = (i_1, i_2, \ldots, i_k, \ldots, i_n)$ assigning different values to issues $\{i_k\}_{1 \leq k \leq n}$. Each issue k takes values in interval $[i_k^{min}, i_k^{max}]$ and its utility u_k is weighted by $w_k \in [0, 1]$. The decomposition of issues $\{i_k\}_{1 \le k \le n}$ into a clusters $\{C_j\}_{1 \le j \le m}$ implies a new representation (Fig. 2).

$$u(o) = \sum_{j=1}^{m} u_{C_j}(s) \qquad (2)$$

with $s \subseteq_j o$, meaning that the sub-utility u_{C_j} is applied to a subset of issues s within cluster C_j. Clusters C_j are lumped together depending on how they affect utility u. Since, the utility (Fig. 1) is linear additive in terms of the issues, we take the assumption that $|C_j| = c, \forall j$ with $c < m$. We take this assumption for the sake of the experimental section as it will be omitted if the shape of the utility (Fig. 1) is unknown or nonlinear. After decomposing their utility spaces, the agents possess the ability to negotiate over sub-bids and reach sub-agreements. The protocol records the results of the sub-agreements and combines the sub-agreements into a complete agreement at the end [2].

In terms of the linear utility functions, the issues can be divided into subsets without any deeper consideration about the interdependency. But it will completely opposite in the case of nonlinear utility functions. Since some issues are bounded together within the utility function, their sub-utilities depend on each other while impacting the global utility. The interdependency should be taken into account when we try to form the sub utility functions. In order to measure the interdependency of the issues, we propose to use a marginal utility loss (MUL) as one criterion. The values of marginal utility loss reflect the impact that the issue clusters have on the global utility.

Formally, let the set of n issues $I = \{i_1, i_2, \ldots, i_k, \ldots, i_n\}$ be defined over domains $\mathcal{D} = \times_{i_k \in I} D_{i_k}$ with D_{i_k} being the domain of issue i_k. For any subset $S \subset I$, we define the sub-domains $\mathcal{D}_S = \times_{i_k \in S} D_{i_k}$. We then define the marginal utility loss (MUL), $\frac{\Delta u}{\Delta S}$, for any given subset of issues S as in (3).

$$\frac{\Delta u}{\Delta S} = \max_{\mathcal{D}_{-S}} \left[\max_{\mathcal{D}_S} u(S, -S) - \min_{\mathcal{D}_S} u(S, -S) \right] \qquad (3)$$

The function $u : I \to [0, 1]$ is the normalized utility function of the agent. The set $-S$ is defined as $-S = I \setminus S$. Each agent will use its MUL to infer the clustering of the issues within its utility function and thus, manage their negotiation agendas according to the interdependency among issues and the induced utility cost.

4 Experiments

As an initial proof of concept, we conducted experiments to prove that even without the complex process of interdependence extraction and utility decomposition, the DaC technique still has its effect on the results of automated negotiations. Then, we applied the same approach to nonlinear domains of negotiation.

4.1 Experimental Settings

Automated negotiating agents are put into use during the experiments for proof of concept. Our simulations were developed using the NegMAS platform to implement and test DAOP. NegMAS supports many protocols and the negotiation is not limited to bilateral cases [22,23]. Moreover, the dynamical feature of NegMAS allow the manipulation of all the parameters that affect the negotiation. In our simulations, we focus on the parameters shown in Table 1.

Table 1. Experimental settings.

Agent strategy	Bidding and accepting
Protocol	DAOP
Number of issues	6
Reservation values	$0.1, 0.2, \ldots, 0.9$
Time limit	50 s
Trials per simulation	100
Utility functions	Linear additive and nonlinear
Dividing strategy	Bids are divided into m subsets

For the nonlinear utility functions, we adopt exponential functions (4) as a specific form of functions that are widely used in the field of economics and finance [7,16]. The weights in (4) can be regarded as part of the agent's disposition to risk aversion.

$$u : I \to [0,1] \tag{4}$$

$$u(o;m) = e^{-\sum_{k=1}^{m} w_k i_k} + e^{-\sum_{k=m+1}^{n} w_k i_k}$$

With outcome $o = (i_1, i_2, \ldots, i_k, \ldots, i_n)$ and variable $m \in [1, n-1]$ referring to the number of partitions of the issues. For a simple exponential utility function involving two issues, the shape is shown in Fig. 4.

With only two issues, the agents may be able to find optimal offers within short time. However, while dealing with more than two issues, the utility shape becomes much more complex and it will take a large amount of time for the agents to reach a win-win agreement without the DaC paradigm.

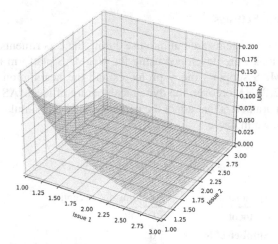

Fig. 4. Utility shape of an exponential utility function

4.2 Agent Settings

In the simulations, we used two agents with the same bidding and acceptance strategies. When the protocol requests the agent to make a proposal to the opponent, the agent first generates an offer randomly from the bidding space, and then proposes it to the opponent. When responding to an offer, the agent evaluates the offer using its utility function, then accepts the offer if its utility is satisfactory with respect to some reservation value, or declines if it is not. Adapted to our DAOP protocol, the agents have the ability to propose partial offers and respond to partial proposals. The offer an agent generates can be converted into a partial offer. Agents use utility functions with quasi-similar structures having different weights $w_k \in [0, 1]$. In the following, the utility functions the agents use for the evaluations will be decomposed with the mechanism we introduced in the previous sections when agents negotiating over subsets of issues.

4.3 Results

In the following, we look at the results given additive linear utility functions and exponential utility functions.

Linear Additive Utility Function. We start by looking at the utility and social welfare values for different numbers of issues. In Fig. 5, when there were only a few issues to negotiate over, the issue space was small enough for the agents to come up with the optimal offer. The agents finally agreed upon high-utilities and high-social welfare agreements. As the number of issues gradually increased, the agents started to offer sub-optimal even bad offers. This directly caused the significant drop of the utilities and social welfare.

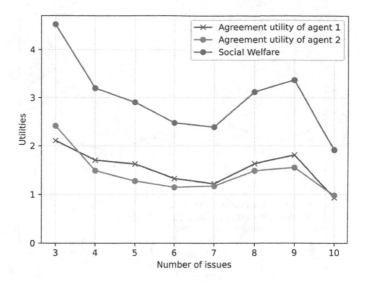

Fig. 5. The individual utilities of the agents and the social welfare decrease with an increasing number of issues

After applying the DaC approach, we obtain Fig. 6. The performances became more stable and the utilities and social welfare of the agents were able to sustain a comparatively higher value.

Moreover, the agents using DaC strategy were able to achieve significantly better social welfares during 100 simulations than the agents without the strategy as shown in Fig. 7.

Nonlinear Utility Function. Unlike the linear case, agents using nonlinear utility functions have specific preferences on the clustering of the issues. However, it is impossible for the agents to accurately model preference structure. The best they can do is to approximate the utility "black boxes" using the decomposition mechanism we introduced in Sect. 3. The marginal utility loss will be used to infer the clustering of the issues to a certain degree.

In Fig. 8, the bars marked in red are the expected proper clustering the agents should infer from the $\frac{\Delta u}{\Delta S}$ value. The marginal utility loss of cluster $\{0, 1, 2\}$ and cluster $\{3, 4, 5\}$ showed a consistent trend because of the original clustering in the utility function. While we vary the values in the issues, the impact of correct clustering is not comparable with the wrong clustering, which is shown by the $\frac{\Delta u}{\Delta S}$ values. The $\frac{\Delta u}{\Delta S}$ values of cluster $\{0, 1, 2\}$ and cluster $\{3, 4, 5\}$ are smaller than other clusters. Comparing with the case of not using the DaC paradigm, another hypothesis is that the agents using the DaC paradigm and marginal utility loss to manage the negotiation agenda should perform better on both time cost and social welfares. The experiment results are shown in the figures.

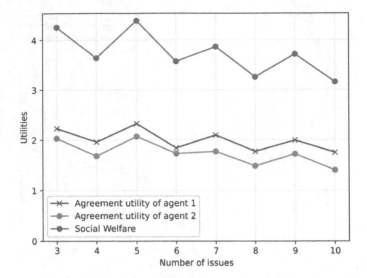

Fig. 6. Applying Divide-and-Conquer (DaC) to utilities

The agents using the DaC paradigm, which are marked as DaC agents, performed better under most cases. While the reservation value of the agents is small, the agents without the DaC paradigm performed as good as the DaC agents. However, when the reservation value became higher and higher, which means the agents became more selective, as the negotiation got more difficult, the utility of the agents without DaC paradigm dramatically dropped. In addition, the DaC agents always performed better on the time they consumed for negotiation, which indicates that the agents found optimal offers faster.

4.4 Discussion

By taking a look at the result, we will know that the DaC algorithm enhances the performances of the agents in terms of the social welfare and time cost. It successfully decomposes the huge utility space into smaller sub utility space so that the automated negotiating agents solve the negotiation problems in a more efficient manner with the DAOP allowing the agents to bid over sub utility space. The marginal utility loss reflects the clustering in the nonlinear utility functions to a degree. It becomes possible to manage the negotiation agendas by applying the marginal utility loss. However, for the future work, we will not only look into the similar trend showed in the social welfare Fig. 5. There are also several possible improvements that can be made with respect to several aspects.

Measurement of the Global Efficiency. From the perspective of environmental settings, it will be useful to measure the relationship of the usage of DaC strategy and the success ratio during negotiation. By looking at and comparing the social welfares,

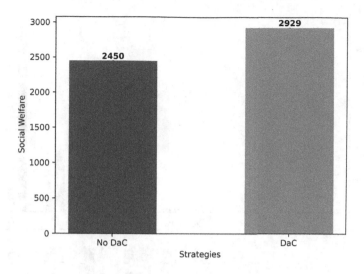

Fig. 7. Social welfare for 100 trials

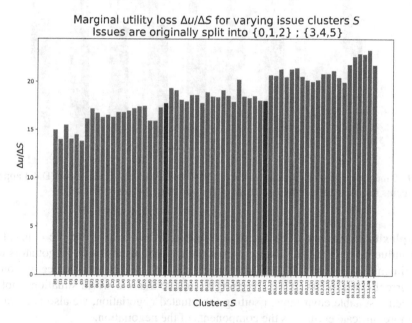

Fig. 8. Marginal utility loss ($\frac{\Delta u}{\Delta S}$) for different issue clusters S with complementary clusters $\{0, 1, 2\}$ and $\{3, 4, 5\}$

time cost and success ratio from both cases, with DaC and without DaC, we should get a better and clearer idea about how DaC strategy benefits our negotiation system. Furthermore, it will be easier to come up with an optimal negotiation setting when dealing with negotiation opponents with different strategies.

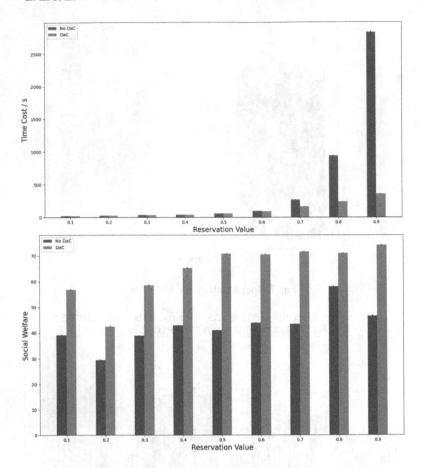

Fig. 9. Time cost and social welfare with and without the divide-and-conquer (DaC) approach. The agents negotiate using nonlinear utilities and variable reservation values

Complexity of Agents. The agents are simple. In order to prove the concept with least influence of other factors, we picked the random agents as the negotiators of the experiments. Apparently, it is not very appropriate to connect realistic negotiation with the current experiments. If we are going to imitate the real-world situations, not only we need a suitable environment setting for situated negotiation, we also need rational and more intricate entities as the components of the negotiation.

Interdependent Issues. In order to further test the effectiveness of DaC algorithm on the interdependent issues based negotiation, in the next step of this research, we will add more constraints to the issue settings to make the issues more interdependent.

5 Conclusion and Future Work

In this paper, we proposed a novel approach using the classical DaC paradigm to cope with the exponential growth of the utility space under complex situations. We first applied the approach to the agents using linear utility functions. The agents' performances were improved with the DaC paradigm. In the case of nonlinear utility functions, which is more realistic, we measure the marginal utility loss of different issue clusters and infer the proper clustering of the interdependent issues. Results show that the approach works under both situations. Future investigations will firstly focus on using different agents and then running the simulations with different domains. Another possible contribution of this work is that our approach also sets the basis for the possibility to combine our DaC protocol with meta-negotiations. The negotiation agendas can be managed through meta-negotiations with the criterions set by our marginal utility loss and thus, the problem of negotiating over a complex and large agenda will be solved. We also believe this is a chance to connect the automated negotiation research with larger range of real-world applications. which as some related applications in many domains [26,30,34].

Acknowledgements. This research was partially supported by JSPS Kakenhi Grant Number JP20K11936, and JST CREST Grant Number JPMJCR20D1.

References

1. Alam, M., Gerding, E.H., Rogers, A., Ramchurn, S.D.: A scalable interdependent multi-issue negotiation protocol for energy exchange. In: Twenty-Fourth International Joint Conference on Artificial Intelligence (2015)
2. Arrow, K.J., Jahnssonin säätiö. Y.: Aspects of the theory of risk-bearing. Economica **33**, 251 (1966)
3. Aydogan, R., Festen, D., Hindriks, K., Jonker. C.: Alternating Offers Protocols for Multilateral Negotiation, vol. 674, pp. 153–167 (2017)
4. Baarslag, T., Hindriks, K., Jonker, C., Kraus, S., Lin, R.: The first automated negotiating agents competition (ANAC 2010). In: New Trends in Agent-Based Complex Automated Negotiations. Studies in Computational Intelligence, vol. 383. Springer, Heidelberg (2010) .https://doi.org/10.1007/978-3-642-24696-8_7
5. Baarslag, T., Kaisers, M.: The value of information in automated negotiation: a decision model for eliciting user preferences. In: Proceedings of the 16th Conference on Autonomous Agents and Multiagent Systems, pp. 391–400 (2017)
6. Bouton, M., Julian, K., Nakhaei, A., Fujimura, K., Kochenderfer, M.J.: Utility decomposition with deep corrections for scalable planning under uncertainty. In: Proceedings of the 17th International Conference on Autonomous Agents and MultiAgent Systems, pp. 462–469 (2018)
7. Choi Chiu, M., Ying Wong, H.: Optimal investment for an insurer with cointegrated assets: CRRA utility. Insur. Math. Econo. **52**(1), 52–64 (2013)
8. Fatima, S., Wooldridge, M., Jennings, N.R.: Optimal agendas for multi-issue negotiation. In: Proceedings of the Second International Joint Conference on Autonomous Agents and Multiagent Systems, AAMAS 2003, pp. 129–136, New York, NY, USA. Association for Computing Machinery (2003)

9. Fujita, K., Ito, T., Klein, M.: An approach to scalable multi-issue negotiation: decomposing the contract space. Comput. Intell. **30**, 02 (2014)
10. Guler, A.U., Demirović, E., Chan, J., Bailey, J., Leckie, C., Stuckey, P.J.: A divide and conquer algorithm for predict+ optimize with non-convex problems. In: Proceedings of the AAAI Conference on Artificial Intelligence, vol. 36, pp. 3749–3757 (2022)
11. Hadfi, R., Ito, T.: Addressing complexity in multi-issue negotiation via utility hypergraphs. In: Proceedings of the AAAI Conference on Artificial Intelligence, vol. 28 (2014)
12. Hadfi, R., Ito, T.: On the complexity of utility hypergraphs. In: Fukuta, N., Ito, T., Zhang, M., Fujita, K., Robu, V. (eds.) Recent Advances in Agent-based Complex Automated Negotiation. SCI, vol. 638, pp. 89–105. Springer, Cham (2016). https://doi.org/10.1007/978-3-319-30307-9_6
13. Hale, J., Kim, P., Gratch, J.: Preference interdependencies in a multi-issue salary negotiation. In: Proceedings of the 22nd ACM International Conference on Intelligent Virtual Agents, pp. 1–8 (2022)
14. Hindriks, K., Jonker, C.M., Kraus, S., Lin, R., Tykhonov. D.: Genius: negotiation environment for heterogeneous agents. In: Proceedings of the 8th International Conference on Autonomous Agents and Multiagent Systems-Vol. 2, pp. 1397–1398 (2009)
15. Ito, T., Hattori, H., Klein, M.: Multi-issue negotiation protocol for agents: exploring non-linear utility spaces. In: Proceedings of the 20th International Joint Conference on Artificial Intelligence, Hyderabad, India, 6–12 January 2007, pp. 1347–1352 (2007)
16. Jaffray, J.-Y.: Linear utility theory for belief functions. Oper. Res. Lett. **8**(2), 107–112 (1989)
17. Jennings, N.R., Faratin, P., Lomuscio, A.R., Parsons, S., Sierra, C., Wooldridge, M.: Automated negotiation: prospects, methods and challenges. Int. J. Group Decis. Negot. **10**(2):199–215 (2001)
18. Kattan, A., Fatima. S.: Evolving optimal agendas and strategies for negotiation in dynamic environments: a surrogate based approach. In: Proceedings of the 14th Annual Conference Companion on Genetic and Evolutionary Computation, pp. 1435–1436 (2012)
19. Kelly, F., Key, P., Walton, N., et al.: Incentivized optimal advert assignment via utility decomposition. In: ACM Conference on Economics and Computation. Citeseer (2014)
20. Kirli, D., et al.: Smart contracts in energy systems: a systematic review of fundamental approaches and implementations. Renew. Sustain. Energy Rev. **158**, 112013 (2022)
21. Maestre, I.M., Lopez-Carmona, M.A., Carral, J.A., Ibanez, G.: A recursive protocol for negotiating contracts under non-monotonic preference structures. Group Decis. Negot. **22**(1), 1–43 (2013)
22. Mohammad, Y., Nakadai, S., Greenwald, A.: NegMAS: a platform for situated negotiations. In: Aydoğan, R., Ito, T., Moustafa, A., Otsuka, T., Zhang, M. (eds.) ACAN 2019. SCI, vol. 958, pp. 57–75. Springer, Singapore (2021). https://doi.org/10.1007/978-981-16-0471-3_4
23. Mohammad, Y., Viqueira, E., Ayerza, N., Greenwald, A., Nakadai, S., Morinaga, S.: Supply Chain Management World, pp. 153–169 (2019)
24. Narayanan, S., Moslemi, R., Pittaluga, F., Liu, B., Chandraker, M.: Divide-and-conquer for lane-aware diverse trajectory prediction. In: Proceedings of the IEEE/CVF Conference on Computer Vision and Pattern Recognition, pp. 15799–15808 (2021)
25. Parkes, D.C. Iterative Combinatorial Auctions. MIT Press, Cambridge (2006)
26. Ros, R., Sierra, C.: A negotiation meta strategy combining trade-off and concession moves. Auton. Agent. Multi-Agent Syst. **12**(2), 163–181 (2006)
27. Sengupta, A., Mohammad, Y., Nakadai, S.: An autonomous negotiating agent framework with reinforcement learning based strategies and adaptive strategy switching mechanism. In: Proceedings of the Thirty-First International Joint Conference on Artificial Intelligence (IJCAI-22) (2021)

28. Simon, H.A.: Bounded rationality. In: Eatwell, J., Milgate, M., Newman, P. (eds.) Utility and Probability, pp. 15–18. Springer, Cham (1990). https://doi.org/10.1007/978-1-349-20568-4_5
29. Smith, D.H.: The design of divide and conquer algorithms. Sci. Comput. Program. **5**, 37–58 (1985)
30. Tang, X., Moustafa, A., Ito, T.: The design of meta-strategy that can obtain higher negotiating efficiency. In: 2018 Thirteenth International Conference on Knowledge, Information and Creativity Support Systems (KICSS)
31. Tversky, A., Kahneman. D.: Judgment under uncertainty: heuristics and biases: Biases in judgments reveal some heuristics of thinking under uncertainty. Science **185**(4157), 1124–1131 (1974)
32. Weiss, G.: Multiagent Systems. MIT Press, Cambridge (2013)
33. Zhang, X.: Klein, M.: Hierarchical negotiation model for complex problems with large-number of interdependent issues. In: 2012 IEEE/WIC/ACM International Conferences on Web Intelligence and Intelligent Agent Technology, vol. 2, pp. 126–133 (2012)
34. Zhang, X., Klein, M., Marsá-Maestre, I.: Scalable complex contract negotiation with structured search and agenda management. In: Proceedings of the National Conference on Artificial Intelligence, vol. 2, pp. 1507–1513, June 2014
35. Zou, Y., et al.: Text semantic matching with disentangled keywords and intents. http://arxiv.org/abs/2203.02898arXiv:2203.02898 (2022)

Concession Strategy Adjustment in Automated Negotiation Problems

Yuchen Liu$^{(\boxtimes)}$, Rafik Hadfi, and Takayuki Ito

Department of Social Informatics, Kyoto University, Kyoto, Japan
liu.yuchen.42h@st.kyoto-u.ac.jp, {rafik.hadfi,ito}@i.kyoto-u.ac.jp

Abstract. Automated negotiation agents usually rely on theories and principles from other fields to guide their concession behavior so that they can perform better when put into productive environments. For example, a marketing agent developed for automated trading could rely on financial theories. While introducing new theories, however, new parameters will be introduced to the agent's concession mechanisms as well. This paper, shows a method for adjusting these parameters to construct a more powerful concession mechanisms. Experiments were done with the Supply Chain Management League (SCML) one-shot environment, and the results indicate that this method can actually improve the performance of agents which employ theories mainly from economic fields. Furthermore, the method can also help distinguish models that are inefficient or even have negative effects in certain situations.

Keywords: Agents · Automated negotiation · Concession · Electronic commerce · Game theory · Multiagent systems · Supply chain

1 Introduction

Intelligent and autonomous can be seen as carriers of Artificial Intelligence (AI). For instance, they sometimes appear in physical forms, such as the ones in robotic networks [16], while in other times they appear as software programs like automatic stock traders [2] and many other applications [9]. Among these applications, automated negotiation is the field that utilises self-interested and rational agents to accomplish negotiation tasks that are originally conducted by humans. In the paper "Automated Negotiation: Prospects, Methods and Challenges" [6] the author defines automated negotiation as containing three key topics: negotiation protocols, negotiation objects, and agent decision models. Based on this definition of automated negotiation, there are many scenarios where automated negotiation could be utilized. The Automated Negotiating Agents Competition (ANAC) is a competition that started in 2010 which focuses on testing automated negotiation strategies and methodologies [7]. There are many sub-competitions in ANAC such as multi-player games like werewolf, diplomacy simulation, and market simulation.

For agents in a negotiating environment, improving their performance to meet certain requirements is essential for them to be considered as rational agents [15]. In this case, it is a smart way to introduce theories and principles from other fields into the agent models. For example, a robotic vacuum cleaner needs knowledge from geometry and fluid mechanics [8] to help it plan its cleaning route; two competing agents want to use game theory as their reference to gain more profit from each other [5]. However, introducing new mechanisms also means introducing complexity, especially with new mechanisms that usually contain new parameter sets. Obviously, how to set these parameters to proper values is a challenge when building new agents.

The Supply Chain Management League (SCML) is a competition where contestants submit their code to represent agents of factories in a supply chain. The aim is to earn more "money" [12]. SCML one-shot track is a simplified version of SCML standard game. In this version, agents do not need to consider long-term plans, but have to concentrate more on negotiation strategies [11,14]. Agents in SCML one-shot games need to negotiate with several of their buyers or sellers to buy raw materials for production, or sell products for money at the same time. The negotiation protocol is simple: agents make offers in turn. When receiving an offer, an agent can choose to accept it or reject it. In case the agent rejects the offer of the other agent, she needs to make a counter-offer, or end the negotiation. One of the most important factors is the concession rate [3,4,10,17], if the concession rate is too high, the agent may lose profits. But if the concession rate is too low, then it is hard to reach an agreement with the partner agents, and thus, no profit at all.

Since SCML is a simulation of a supply chain, in other words, a simulation of a market, some financial principles could be utilized. And it is a great example as mentioned above, for agents in a competitive environment and agents have a utility function which considers money earned as an agent's utility. In the following sections we will illustrate what theory and mechanism an agent could adopt to adjust the concession rate, what parameters would be introduced, and most importantly, how these parameters could be tuned to improve the performance of the agent. The method we are going to introduce was used when developing the "UCOneshotAgent" agent which is the third place (tie) winner of the SCML competition (one-shot track) in 2021.

The paper is structured as follows. In Sect. 2, we will introduce what theories we will adopt and what parameters need to be embedded into the concession strategy. In Sect. 3, we will introduce our tuning strategy, that is, how we can adjust the parameters to improve agent's rationality. Finally, in Sect. 4, we will conduct some experiments using the method specified in Sect. 3 to adjust the agent defined in Sect. 2 to see if the agent performance improved or not.

2   Parameters of Agents

Let us start by specifying the basic behaviours an agent should adopt in SCML one-shot environment. Consider a traditional one-to-one negotiation scenario, where two agents take turns in exchanging offers, accept the offers, refuse and present a counter-offer, or end the negotiation. Usually, an agent will start with an offer which maximize its utility function and this offer is unlikely to be accepted by the partner agent. A rule of thumb is to gradually reduce one's utility so that an agreement is reached quickly. In the SCML scenario, the gain on one side can only be obtained on the expense of the other side. In this case, the buyer wants a lower price while the seller wants a higher price. The parameters will be built from the basic concession strategy aspects: concession rate, starting utility, minimum acceptable utility. And the concession strategy could be expressed with the Eq. (1).

$$U(t) = (U_{Max} - U_{Min})\left(\frac{T_{Total} - t}{T_{Total}}\right)^{E} + U_{Min} \tag{1}$$

where U is the utility value at time t, U_{Max} is the maximum utility that could be obtained from the offer, U_{Min} is the minimum acceptable utility that could be obtained from the offer, T_{Total} is the total negotiation time, and which can be discrete (steps) or continuous (time interval). Finally, E is the concession rate, with higher values meaning that the agent will concede quicker.

Using a utility function with a concession parameter is not enough. To make more profit, we have to consider the characteristics of the partner agents. If an partner agent is tough and unwilling to concede too much, we have to raise our concession rate to make sure that an agreement can be reached before time runs out. Likewise, if a partner agent is easy to compromise, we want to lower the concession rate to make more profit. However, we do not know how our partner agents will be implemented, so, it is a good idea to adjust the concession rate after each turn based on the negotiation steps and results with a certain partner agent. Specifically, if the agreement was reached in a few steps then the partner agent should be willing to accept, thus, our concession rate should be lower for the next turn. If the agreement was reached in a reasonable number of steps, the concession rate should be kept unchanged. Finally, if the negotiation took too many steps or failed, then the concession rate should be adjusted higher, for our partner agent must be a tough one. Based on this strategy, we need a learning rate to specify how much we add to or subtract from the concession rate.

Moving to the general perspective, the strategies mentioned above focus more on one-to-one negotiation scenarios. But SCML one-shot game is a many-to-many trade simulator, this means that each agent has several partner and competitor agents. If we consider the concepts "buyer's market" and "seller's market" which illustrate that if the number of agents at a level of the supply chain is low, they tend to become more aggressive by reducing buying price and rising selling price, and vice versa. In a one-shot game, agents are assigned to two levels [12]. The numbers of agents in level 0 (L0) and level 1 (L1) are assigned randomly when the game starts, thus, this principle can be utilized to adjust agent's offering prices.

Until this point, we have dug out parameters such utility values U_{Max}, U_{Min}, the concession rate E, the adjusted rate of concession based on negotiation history and the adjusted rate of concession based on #L1/#L0 (number of L1 agents divided by number of L0 agents). Some of the parameters are based on basic automated negotiation theories, some are coming from commerce principles, and others were driven from the perspective of concurrent processing. In the next stage, these parameters could be tuned to improve the performance of the agents.

3   Parameter Tuning Strategy

In the previous section, we discussed a concession negotiation strategy and some parameters that can be applied to this strategy. The next step is to adjust these parameters to maximize agent's performance. The basic idea of parameter tuning is to run simulations with other agents, recording results, adjusting parameters and running simulations again to see if the agent has better performance.

First of all, all parameters have to have a range, for example, the concession rate should be greater than 0 to make it a cooperator rather than a competitor as illustrated in the book "What to Bid and When to Stop"; other parameters such as concession adjustment parameters (#L1/#L0 ratio adjustment and negotiation history adjustment) should not be too large for that may cause the agent to behave in a strange way.

Next, we need to find some agents for training. Fortunately, the official SCML Python package provides sample agents. These agents' parameters could be adjusted into many versions to increase the simulation environment's diversity. It is also a good idea to utilize agents from the competition of 2021.

The turning process is illustrated in Fig. 1. At the beginning, all parameters will randomly get an initial value. Each set of parameters will be evaluated by running simulations with other agents, then the score of the set will be stored. Next, one of the parameters inside the set will be adjusted by a fixed positive or negative learning rate. If a new set is able to achieve a higher score than the older set, then the new set is maintained, otherwise the old set will be restored. When there is no improvement for a certain number of rounds or there are no new sets available, the whole tuning process finishes. There are two variables in the turning process that need some extra attention. First, the learning rate l, which decides the speed of tuning, but it should not be too large for parameters may miss the best point. Second, the tolerance τ, to set a limit of parameter set adjusting, if the program cannot find a better set within a certain number of rounds, the best set will be treated as the final result.

4   Experiments

4.1   Settings of Experiments

The test environment is based on Python 3.8 with packages: scml, scml-agents, and NegMAS [13]. The charts were generated by matplotlib. The list of the parameters is the following.

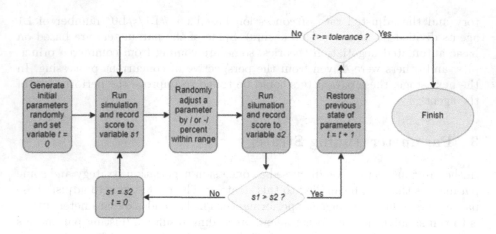

Fig. 1. Flow chart of tuning process

- The initial concession rate: $C \in [0.05, 1.0]$
- The maximum utility (price): $U_{Max} \in [0.75, 1.0]$
- The minimum utility (price): $U_{Min} \in [0.0, 0.25]$
- The negotiation history adjustment factor: $F_{his} \in [0.001, 0.01]$. If negotiation successes/fails in 0-5, 6-10, 11-15, 16-20 turns concession rate will be adjusted by $[\pm1.5, \pm1.0, \pm0.5, 0] * F_{his}$.
- The #L1/#L0 ratio adjustment factor, namely $F_r \in [0.1, 0.6]$. Applied after F_{his}, concession rate will be adjusted with the formula: $C' = C \times (\frac{\#L1}{\#L0})^{F_r}$ if the agent belongs to L1 else $C' = C \times (\frac{\#L0}{\#L1})^{F_r}$.

For the competitor agents, we have chosen "BetterAgent", "AdaptiveAgent" and "LearningAgent" from SCML's online documentation with different concession rates. Together with some agents from 2021's SCML competition, including "Agent74", "GodFather" and "PDPSyncAgent" [1]. Since there is no standard benchmark tool, we had to construct a test environment by ourselves. To avoid overfit each epoch a set of new agents will be generated.

4.2   Results of Experiments

In the first experiment, we followed the steps illustrated in Fig. 1, the initial parameters were set to $C : 0.95$, $U_{Max} : 0.8289$, $U_{Min} : 0.2237$, $F_{his} : 0.0067$, $F_r : 0.3895$, With these parameters, we got a score of 0.8435. Then we did the tuning process with $\tau : 10$ and $l = 5\%$ where each tuning will be plus or minus 5% of its range size. After tuning, the score increased to 1.0271 as Fig. 2 (left) shows. Finally, the parameter set becomes $C : 0.95$, $U_{Max} : 0.8289$, $U_{Min} : 0.2237$, $F_{his} : 0.0062$, and $F_r : 0.2842$. Actually, the score does improve a lot but it seems that parameters did not get to much adjustment, only F_r had some changes. From the graph we can see that the score reached its maximum at round 16, but it cannot make further improvements by adding or subtracting to any parameters, in other words, it probably reached a local minimum.

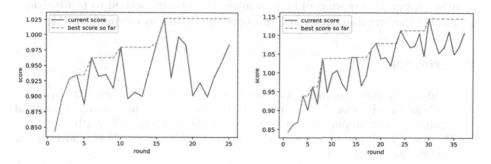

Fig. 2. Line chart of first Experiment (left) and second Experiment (right)

To solve this problem, a simple strategy can be adopted as to make the program have a large learning rate at the beginning and reduce it as the number of rounds grows. Let us start at the same point as the first Experiment, but set $l = 32\%$ and reduce it by half every 10 rounds while keep τ unchanged. As Fig. 2 (right) shows, this strategy helps the agent to achieve an even better score of 1.1455, and the final parameter set is $C : 0.95, U_{Max} : 0.7601, U_{Min} : 0.0, F_{his} : 0.001, F_r : 0.3070$. And I think other local search techniques may also helpful such as beam search.

5 Discussion and Conclusion

As the experiments show, the performance of an agent rose a lot after parameter tuning, especially in the second experiment. The tuning process can help find some redundant theories. In the second experiment, we see that after parameter tuning, the parameter U_{min} became zero, which means the introduction of such a theory will have a negative effect on the overall performance of our agent, so, it should be removed, at least in this kind of environment.

However, this method has some disadvantages and limitations. Firstly, this tuning process must be based on other mechanisms which need to be concluded from the specific problem and/or principles from other subjects (like the buyer's/seller's market). Next, we can see that the graphs in Fig. 2 is not smooth, this is because the simulation process is not stable especially when the number of simulation rounds is small This character prolongs the time required by this method making it not very effective and may introduce some uncertainties. But still, this tuning strategy could be applied not only to SCML one-shot game but to other similar automated negotiation scenarios.

In future research, we would like to concentrate more on improving the efficiency when using the tuning technique in this paper. For example, we would try using several threads each starting with different parameter sets. We also want to find strategies for stable and unstable environments (this can be illustrated as the variance of the score an agent is able to achieve in a simulation run). Another orientation is we could try to apply the tuning method to utility-based agents in other environments, and not only to concession mechanisms [15].

References

1. Scml-agents. https://github.com/yasserfarouk/scml-agents. Accessed 27 Apr 2022
2. Abduljabbar, P., Dia, H., Liyanage, S., Bagloee, S.A.: Applications of artificial intelligence in transport: an overview. Sustainability 11(1), 189 (2019)
3. Baarslag, T.: What to bid and when to stop. Ph.D. thesis, Delft University of Technology (2014)
4. Baarslag, T., Hindriks, K., Jonker, C.: Towards a quantitative concession-based classification method of negotiation strategies. In: Kinny, D., Hsu, J.Y., Governatori, G., Ghose, A.K. (eds.) PRIMA 2011. LNCS (LNAI), vol. 7047, pp. 143–158. Springer, Heidelberg (2011). https://doi.org/10.1007/978-3-642-25044-6_13
5. Gibbons, R., et al.: A Primer in Game Theory. University of Manchester (1992)
6. Jennings, N.R., Faratin, P., Lomuscio, A.R., Parsons, S., Sierra, C., Wooldridge, M.: Automated negotiation: prospects, methods and challenges. Int. J. Group Decis. Negoti. 10(2), 199–215 (2001)
7. Jonker, C., Aydogan, R., Baarslag, T., Fujita, K., Ito, T., Hindriks, K.: Automated negotiating agents competition (ANAC). In: Proceedings of the AAAI Conference on Artificial Intelligence, vol. 31 (2017)
8. Lai, X., Wang, H., Liu, H.: Research on duct flow field optimisation of a robot vacuum cleaner. Int. J. Adv. Rob. Syst. 8(5), 65 (2011)
9. Liu, Y., Wang, Y., Li, Y., Gooi, H.B., Xin, H.: Multi-agent based optimal scheduling and trading for multi-microgrids integrated with urban transportation networks. IEEE Trans. Power Syst. 36(3), 2197–2210 (2020)
10. Lopes, F., Coelho, H.: Concession behaviour in automated negotiation. In: Buccafurri, F., Semeraro, G. (eds.) EC-Web 2010. LNBIP, vol. 61, pp. 184–194. Springer, Heidelberg (2010). https://doi.org/10.1007/978-3-642-15208-5_17
11. Mirzayi, S., Taghiyareh, F., Nassiri-Mofakham, F.: An opponent-adaptive strategy to increase utility and fairness in agents' negotiation. Appl. Intell. 52(4), 3587–3603 (2022)
12. Mohammad, Y., Areyan Viqueira, E., Alvarez Ayerza, N., Greenwald, A., Nakadai, S., Morinaga, S.: Supply chain management world. In: International Conference on Principles and Practice of Multi-agent Systems, pp. 153–169. Springer, Heidelberg (2019). https://doi.org/10.1007/978-3-540-74512-9_2
13. Mohammad, Y., Nakadai, S., Greenwald, A.: NegMAS: a platform for situated negotiations. In: Aydoğan, R., Ito, T., Moustafa, A., Otsuka, T., Zhang, M. (eds.) ACAN 2019. SCI, vol. 958, pp. 57–75. Springer, Singapore (2021). https://doi.org/10.1007/978-981-16-0471-3_4
14. Renting, B.M., Hoos, H.H., Jonker, C.M.: Automated configuration of negotiation strategies. arXiv preprint arXiv:2004.00094 (2020)
15. Russell, S.: Artificial Intelligence: A Modern Approach, 4th edn. Prentice Hall, Hoboken (2021)

16. Vorotnikov, S., Ermishin, K., Nazarova, A., Yuschenko, A.: Multi-agent robotic systems in collaborative robotics. In: Ronzhin, A., Rigoll, G., Meshcheryakov, R. (eds.) ICR 2018. LNCS (LNAI), vol. 11097, pp. 270–279. Springer, Cham (2018). https://doi.org/10.1007/978-3-319-99582-3_28
17. Williams, C.R., Robu, V., Gerding, E.H., Jennings, N.R.: Using Gaussian processes to optimise concession in complex negotiations against unknown opponents. In: Twenty-Second International Joint Conference on Artificial Intelligence (2011)

Author Index

Printed in the United States
by Baker & Taylor Publisher Services

Printed in the United States
by Baker & Taylor Publisher Services